THE FUTURE IS NOW

Exploring the Cutting Edge of Technology

I0478191

Hey there, after diving into this book, you'll gain a solid grasp of important technologies, be able to predict upcoming trends, and feel confident when making informed choices in today's ever-changing world.

Mritunjay Kumar Jha

Publisher: Amazon Kindle Direct Publishing
ISBN:
Publication Date:
Edition: First Edition
Cover Design: Mritunjay Kumar Jha
Printed in:

Disclaimer: The information contained in this book is for educational purposes only. While every effort has been made to ensure the accuracy of the content, the author and publisher make no representations or warranties regarding the accuracy, applicability, or completeness of the information presented. Readers are encouraged to do their own research when making decisions based on the information provided in this book.

Mritunjay Kumar Jha

Introduction

We stand at the precipice of an unprecedented era, defined by exponential technological advancements that are rewriting the rules of our world. From artificial intelligence that rivals human intelligence to quantum computers capable of unlocking the universe's secrets, the future we once dreamt of is rapidly becoming our reality. "The Future is Now" is a comprehensive exploration of this transformative landscape, a journey through the cutting-edge innovations that are shaping our present and will define our future. This book is not merely a collection of facts and figures; it's a narrative that invites you to witness first-hand the power of technology to solve some of our most pressing challenges and create a world that is more sustainable, equitable, and prosperous. We will delve into the mysteries of artificial intelligence, unravelling the intricate workings of machine learning and neural networks, and exploring its impact on industries like healthcare, transportation, and entertainment. We will venture into the realm of quantum computing, where the laws of quantum mechanics are harnessed to unlock computational power beyond anything we have ever known, with the potential to revolutionize medicine, materials science, and cryptography. We will explore the innovative solutions to our energy crisis, from harnessing the power of the sun and wind to the promise of hydrogen fuel cells. And we will embark on a journey into the transformative world of biotechnology, where genetic engineering, synthetic biology, and personalized medicine hold the potential to reshape healthcare and redefine our understanding of life itself. But this is not just a celebration of technological progress. We will also grapple with the ethical and societal implications of these ground breaking advancements, examining the challenges they pose to our values, our privacy, and our very existence. Join us as we navigate this exhilarating and complex landscape, exploring the possibilities and perils of a future that is already here.

Contents

Conclusion

Chapter One

The Age of Artificial Intelligence

Understanding AI and Machine Learning

Artificial intelligence (AI) has become an omnipresent force, silently weaving its way into the fabric of our daily lives. From the personalized recommendations we receive on streaming services to the sophisticated algorithms that power our smartphones, AI is revolutionizing the way we live, work, and interact with the world around us. At its core, AI encompasses the creation of intelligent machines capable of performing tasks that typically require human intelligence, such as learning, problem-solving, and decision-making. However, the term "artificial intelligence" is often used interchangeably with "machine learning," which is a subset of AI. Machine learning focuses on the development of algorithms that allow computers to learn from data without explicit programming. These algorithms can identify patterns, make predictions, and even improve their performance over time. Imagine you want to teach a computer to recognize a cat in a photo. You could spend years writing code to define all the features of a cat, from its fur to its whiskers. But with machine learning, you simply feed the computer a massive dataset of images, some labelled as "cat" and others as "not cat." The algorithm will analyse these images, identifying patterns and correlations, and eventually learn to distinguish cats from other objects. This is the essence of machine learning: allowing computers to learn from data, much like humans do. One of the most powerful tools in machine learning is the neural network. Inspired by the structure of the human brain, neural networks consist of interconnected nodes, or neurons, that process and transmit information. Each neuron receives inputs from other neurons and applies a mathematical function to produce an output. By stacking multiple layers of these neurons, neural networks can learn complex relationships and solve problems that traditional algorithms struggle with. Neural networks are particularly adept at tasks like image recognition, natural language processing, and speech recognition. For example, facial recognition systems used in security and social media platforms rely heavily on neural networks to identify individuals from images. Similarly, Chabots that can understand and respond to human language rely on neural networks to process and generate text. The power of machine learning algorithms and neural networks lies in their ability to learn and adapt. As they are exposed to more data, they become more accurate and efficient. This iterative learning process, known as "training," is essential for improving the performance of AI systems. However, AI is not without its challenges. One of the biggest concerns is the potential for bias in algorithms. Machine learning algorithms are trained on data, and if that data reflects existing biases, the algorithms can perpetuate those biases. This has implications for areas like hiring, loan applications, and criminal justice, where biased algorithms can lead to unfair outcomes. Another concern is the lack of transparency in how AI systems make decisions. The complex nature of neural networks often makes it difficult to understand the reasoning behind their outputs. This opacity can raise concerns about accountability and trustworthiness, particularly in applications where decisions have serious consequences. Despite these challenges, AI has the potential to revolutionize countless industries and aspects of our lives. From improving medical diagnoses to developing new materials, AI is already making a tangible impact. As the technology continues to evolve, it is crucial to address the ethical and societal implications of its development and deployment, ensuring that AI is used responsibly and benefits all of humanity. In the next chapter, we will explore the ground breaking advancements of quantum computing, a technology with the potential to surpass even the most powerful AI systems. But for now, let's delve deeper into the world of AI and its transformative impact on healthcare, transportation, and entertainment.

AI in Healthcare

The healthcare industry is one of the most promising frontiers for AI applications. Machine learning algorithms are already being used to analyze vast amounts of patient data, aiding doctors in making more informed diagnoses and treatment plans. One of the most exciting applications of AI in healthcare is in the area of predictive analytics. By analyzing patient data such as medical history, genetic information, and lifestyle factors, AI can identify individuals at risk for specific diseases. This early detection can lead to more timely interventions and potentially save lives. For example, AI algorithms are being used to predict the risk of heart attacks, strokes, and even cancer. These algorithms can consider a range of factors, including age, gender, family history, smoking status, and cholesterol levels, to assess an individual's risk profile. AI is also transforming drug discovery and development. By analyzing massive datasets of chemical compounds and biological targets, AI can identify potential drug candidates and predict their effectiveness and safety. This process can significantly speed up and streamline the drug discovery process, ultimately leading to the development of new treatments for diseases that are currently difficult to treat. AI is not only changing the way we diagnose and treat diseases; it's also revolutionizing medical imaging analysis. Machine learning algorithms can analyze medical images, such as X-rays, CT scans, and MRIs, with high accuracy and speed. This allows radiologists to identify subtle abnormalities that might be missed by the human eye, improving the accuracy of diagnoses and potentially leading to earlier interventions. In addition to diagnosis and treatment, AI is playing an increasing role in robotic surgery. Robots assisted by AI can perform complex surgical procedures with precision and minimal invasiveness. This technology is particularly promising for minimally invasive surgery, allowing surgeons to operate with smaller incisions and reduced recovery times. The use of AI in healthcare raises ethical considerations, such as data privacy and security, the potential for algorithmic bias, and the impact on the doctor-patient relationship. It is essential to ensure that AI is used responsibly and ethically in healthcare, promoting patient well-being and ensuring equitable access to healthcare services.

AI in Transport

The transportation industry is on the cusp of a major transformation, driven by the advancements in autonomous vehicle technology. AI algorithms are at the heart of self-driving cars, enabling them to perceive their surroundings, navigate roads, and make decisions in real-time. Autonomous vehicles hold the potential to revolutionize transportation, offering numerous benefits. They can reduce traffic accidents caused by human error, improve traffic flow, and enhance accessibility for people with disabilities. Moreover, they can reduce emissions and contribute to a more sustainable transportation system. AI is also transforming the entertainment industry, personalizing our experiences in ways that were unimaginable just a few years ago. Streaming services like Netflix and Spotify use AI algorithms to analyze our viewing and listening habits, predicting what we might enjoy and recommending personalized content. Personalized entertainment experiences go beyond just recommendations. AI is being used to create interactive games, personalized music compositions, and immersive virtual reality experiences. AI-powered virtual assistants are becoming increasingly sophisticated, offering personalized recommendations and assistance with tasks such as setting reminders, ordering food, and controlling home devices. The rise of AI-generated content is another exciting development in the entertainment industry. AI algorithms can now generate realistic images, videos, and even music, blurring the lines between human creativity and machine intelligence. This technology has the potential to enhance storytelling, create new forms of art, and democratize access to creative tools. However, the use of AI in transportation and entertainment also raises ethical questions. For example, concerns about the potential for job displacement in the transportation industry, the implications of personalized content for privacy and bias, and the potential for AI-generated content to be used for malicious purposes. As AI continues to transform the world around us, it is crucial to engage in thoughtful discussions about its ethical implications, ensuring that this powerful technology is developed and deployed responsibly. In the next chapter, we will explore the future of AI, examining the potential for even more transformative advancements and the societal impacts of these developments. AI in Healthcare The world of healthcare is undergoing a remarkable transformation, driven by the rapid advancements in artificial intelligence (AI). AI is no longer confined to the realm of science fiction; it's now a powerful tool used by healthcare professionals to diagnose diseases, personalize treatments, and improve patient outcomes. Imagine a future where AI algorithms can analyze your medical history, genetic information, and lifestyle factors to predict your risk of developing specific diseases. This predictive power allows healthcare providers to intervene early, potentially preventing illnesses or catching them at an earlier, more treatable stage. This is the promise of AI powered predictive analytics in healthcare. AI-powered diagnostic tools are revolutionizing how diseases are detected and diagnosed. These tools can analyze medical images, such as X-rays, CT scans, and MRIs, with incredible accuracy, often surpassing human capabilities. For instance, AI algorithms are being used to detect tumours in mammograms, identify abnormalities in retinal scans, and assist radiologists in interpreting complex medical imagery. Beyond diagnosis, AI is also changing how treatments are delivered. AI-powered robotic surgery is becoming increasingly common, offering surgeons greater precision, minimally invasive procedures, and faster recovery times. These robotic systems are equipped with advanced instruments and sensors that allow surgeons to perform intricate operations with unparalleled dexterity. Moreover, AI is enabling the development of personalized medicine, where treatments are tailored to individual patients based on their unique genetic makeup and medical history. AI algorithms can analyze vast datasets of genomic information to identify specific mutations or genetic variations that could influence drug responses. This personalized approach allows doctors to prescribe the most effective medications for each patient, optimizing outcomes and minimizing side effects. AI is also transforming the way healthcare is delivered by automating routine tasks and improving operational efficiency. AI-powered Chabots are being used to answer patient questions, schedule appointments, and provide basic medical advice, freeing up doctors to focus on more complex cases. Furthermore, AI is playing a crucial role in drug discovery and development. By analyzing massive amounts of data on chemical compounds and biological targets, AI can accelerate the identification of potential drug candidates, shortening the time it takes to bring new medications to market. However, the integration of AI in healthcare also raises ethical concerns that must be carefully considered. For instance, the use of AI algorithms in decision-making processes raises questions about bias and fairness. It's essential to ensure that AI systems are trained on diverse datasets and are not perpetuating existing societal inequalities. Another critical ethical concern is data privacy. The vast amounts of personal health information used to train AI systems must be protected rigorously to prevent misuse or unauthorized access. Robust data privacy regulations and safeguards are crucial to ensure that AI in healthcare is used ethically and responsibly. Despite these challenges, the potential benefits of AI in healthcare are undeniable. AI has the power to revolutionize how diseases are diagnosed, treatments are delivered, and healthcare systems are managed. As AI technology continues to evolve, we can expect even more transformative applications in healthcare, leading to improved patient outcomes, enhanced efficiency, and a more equitable healthcare system for all. Let's delve deeper into some specific examples of how AI is transforming healthcare, highlighting its real-world impact. Case Study: AI-Powered Predictive Analytics in Cancer Screening Imagine a world where AI can predict your risk of developing cancer years before any symptoms appear. This is becoming a reality with the development of AI-powered predictive analytics models that can analyze your medical history, genetic information, and lifestyle factors to identify individuals at high risk of developing cancer. For example, a research team at the University of California, San Francisco, developed an AI algorithm that can predict the risk of developing breast cancer in women with high accuracy. The algorithm analyzes a combination of factors, including age, family history, breast density, and genetic mutations, to assess an individual's risk. This information allows doctors to recommend more frequent screenings or preventive measures, potentially catching cancers at an earlier, more treatable stage. Similar AI algorithms are being developed for other cancers, including prostate cancer, colorectal cancer, and lung cancer. These predictive tools have the potential to significantly reduce cancer mortality rates by enabling early detection and intervention. Case Study: AI-Assisted Diagnosis in Radiology Radiologists are tasked with interpreting complex medical images, such as X-rays, CT scans, and MRIs, to detect abnormalities and diagnose diseases. This is a demanding and time-consuming task, and even experienced radiologists can miss subtle signs of disease. AI is emerging as a powerful tool to assist radiologists in their work. AI algorithms can analyze medical images with remarkable accuracy, identifying subtle patterns that may escape human eyes. For example, an AI system developed by Google Health has shown remarkable accuracy in detecting breast cancer in mammograms, often surpassing human radiologists. This AI-powered diagnostic tool can help radiologists make more accurate and timely diagnoses, ultimately leading to better patient outcomes. Case Study: AI-Powered Robotic Surgery in Orthopaedics Robotics are revolutionizing the field of orthopaedic surgery, offering surgeons greater precision and minimally invasive procedures. Robotic surgery systems, such as the da Vinci Surgical System, are equipped with advanced instruments and cameras that allow surgeons to perform complex surgeries with unparalleled dexterity. For example, in knee replacement surgeries, robotic systems can assist surgeons in making precise cuts and implanting the prosthetic knee joint with greater accuracy. This results in a more natural range of motion and faster recovery times for patients. Robotic surgery is also being used in other orthopaedic procedures, including hip replacement, spinal fusion, and fracture repair. These systems offer significant advantages over traditional surgical techniques, including reduced blood loss, shorter hospital stays, and faster recovery times. Case Study: AI-Driven Drug Discovery in Pharmaceutical Research The pharmaceutical industry is embracing AI to accelerate drug discovery and development. AI algorithms can analyze vast datasets of chemical compounds and biological targets, identifying potential drug candidates that would otherwise be missed. For instance, an AI system developed by the pharmaceutical company AstraZeneca has been able to identify new drug candidates for treating Parkinson's disease. The system analyzed millions of chemical compounds and identified potential drugs that can target specific proteins involved in the disease. AI is also being used to optimize clinical trials, reducing the time and cost of bringing new drugs to market. By analyzing patient data and identifying potential biomarkers, AI can help researchers select the most appropriate patients for clinical trials, ensuring that trials are more efficient and successful. The Future of AI in Healthcare The future of AI in healthcare is bright and promising. As AI technology continues to evolve, we can expect even more transformative applications, including: - Personalized medicine: AI will play an increasingly important role in developing personalized medicine approaches, tailoring treatments to individual patients based on their unique genetic makeup and medical history. - AI-powered diagnostics: AI-assisted diagnostic tools will become more sophisticated, enabling early detection of diseases and improving patient outcomes. - Remote healthcare: AI will empower healthcare professionals to provide remote patient monitoring and virtual consultations, expanding access to care in underserved communities. - Drug discovery and development: AI will continue to revolutionize the pharmaceutical industry, accelerating the discovery and development of new drugs and therapies. - Medical education: AI will play a crucial role in training future healthcare professionals, providing immersive simulations and personalized learning experiences. As AI technology continues to advance, we can anticipate a future where AI is an integral part of healthcare, improving patient care, enhancing efficiency, and making healthcare more accessible and equitable for all. However, it's important to acknowledge the ethical considerations and potential challenges that come with integrating AI into healthcare. It is imperative that we develop robust safeguards to ensure that AI is used responsibly, ethically, and for the benefit of all. By embracing AI while addressing these concerns, we can unlock its transformative potential and create a healthier future for generations to come. AI in Transportation and Entertainment Imagine a world where cars drive themselves, seamlessly navigating complex urban landscapes, guided by the invisible hand of artificial intelligence (AI). Picture a future where entertainment is tailored to your unique preferences, with movies, music, and games curated just for you. This is not science fiction; it's the reality AI is rapidly shaping. In the realm of transportation, AI is revolutionizing how we get around. Autonomous vehicles (AVs), equipped with sophisticated AI systems, are poised to transform our roads and cities. These vehicles use a combination of sensors, cameras, and powerful algorithms to perceive their surroundings, make decisions, and navigate safely. Imagine a future where traffic jams become a thing of the past. AVs, communicating with each other, can optimize traffic flow, reducing congestion and improving efficiency. Imagine a world where accidents caused by human error are minimized, leading to safer roads and fewer fatalities. Beyond road transportation, AI is transforming the skies. Drone delivery services are becoming increasingly commonplace, using AI to navigate complex aerial pathways and deliver goods efficiently. AI is even being used to develop advanced air traffic control systems, optimizing flight paths and reducing delays. But the impact of AI in transportation extends far beyond the realm of vehicles. AI-powered logistics platforms are optimizing supply chains, ensuring goods move smoothly and efficiently from point A to point B. AI is also being used to develop intelligent transportation systems, helping cities manage traffic flow, optimize public transportation routes, and create safer and more sustainable urban environments. The entertainment industry is also experiencing a dramatic shift driven by AI. Streaming services, powered by sophisticated algorithms, personalize your entertainment experiences, recommending movies, TV shows, and music tailored to your tastes. AI-powered virtual assistants, like Siri and Alexa, are becoming our personal entertainment guides, curating our entertainment experiences based on our preferences and past behavior. The rise of AI is ushering in a new era of interactive entertainment. Gaming is being revolutionized with AIpowered opponents that adapt to your gameplay, providing a truly immersive and challenging experience. AI is also enhancing the realism and interactivity of virtual reality (VR) and augmented reality (AR) applications, blurring the lines between the digital and physical worlds. The potential of AI in entertainment is vast. AI-powered content generators can create new music, stories, and even artwork, pushing the boundaries of creativity. AI can even be used to analyze audience reactions, helping creators understand what resonates with their audience and creating content that is more engaging and impactful. However, the use of AI in entertainment raises important ethical questions. As algorithms become increasingly sophisticated, concerns about bias and the potential for manipulation arise. We need to be mindful of the impact these technologies have on our creative expression and ensure that AI-powered entertainment tools are used responsibly and ethically. AI's role in transportation and entertainment is just the tip of the iceberg. As AI technology continues to advance, we can expect to see even more transformative applications that will reshape our lives and the world around us. This is a time of incredible innovation, and it's crucial that we approach these advancements with both excitement and a sense of responsibility, ensuring that AI benefits all of humanity.

Ethical Considerations of AI

As AI continues to evolve at an unprecedented pace, its transformative potential is undeniable. However, alongside its remarkable capabilities, AI raises profound ethical questions that demand careful consideration. These ethical considerations are not merely abstract philosophical debates; they have tangible consequences for individuals, society, and the future of our planet. One of the most pressing ethical challenges posed by AI is the issue of privacy. AI systems are increasingly reliant on vast amounts of personal data to function effectively. From our online activity to our medical records, AI algorithms are constantly analyzing and processing our information. While this data can be used to personalize our experiences and improve services, it also raises serious concerns about data breaches, misuse, and the erosion of individual privacy. Imagine a world where you're every move, every online interaction, and every medical detail is tracked and analyzed by AI systems. This raises questions about who has access to this information, how it is being used, and whether individuals have sufficient control over their own data. Another crucial ethical issue is the potential for job displacement. As AI becomes more sophisticated, it is increasingly capable of automating tasks that were previously performed by humans. This raises concerns about widespread job losses in various sectors, from manufacturing to customer service. While AI can create new jobs in fields like AI development and data analysis, the transition can be challenging for individuals who lose their livelihoods. The ethical implications extend beyond individual hardship; they encompass the broader societal impacts of economic inequality and social unrest. How can we ensure that the benefits of AI are shared equitably and that those who are displaced by automation are adequately supported? Beyond privacy and job displacement, AI also poses ethical dilemmas in areas like bias, accountability, and autonomous decision-making. AI systems are trained on data sets that often reflect the biases and prejudices prevalent in society. This can lead to AI systems that perpetuate discrimination and inequality, for example, in areas like criminal justice and loan applications. The question of accountability also becomes complex when AI systems make decisions that have significant consequences for individuals. Who is responsible when an AI system makes a mistake? If an autonomous vehicle causes an accident, who is liable – the manufacturer, the user, or the AI itself? The ethical considerations surrounding AI are not simply abstract philosophical dilemmas; they are real-world issues that demand practical solutions. As we navigate the age of artificial intelligence, we must actively engage in open discussions, develop robust ethical frameworks, and ensure that AI development and deployment are guided by principles of fairness, transparency, and accountability. This requires collaboration between policymakers, technologists, ethicists, and the public to ensure that AI benefits all of humanity while mitigating potential risks. The ethical considerations of AI are not merely abstract philosophical dilemmas; they are real-world issues that demand practical solutions. As we navigate the age of artificial intelligence, we must actively engage in open discussions, develop robust ethical frameworks, and ensure that AI development and deployment are guided by principles of fairness, transparency, and accountability. This requires collaboration between policymakers, technologists, ethicists, and the public to ensure that AI benefits all of humanity while mitigating potential risks. One key approach to address ethical concerns is to promote transparency and accountability in AI systems. This includes making the algorithms used in AI systems more transparent, providing explanations for their decisions, and allowing for human oversight of AI systems that make critical decisions. By making AI systems more transparent and accountable, we can reduce the potential for bias, discrimination, and unintended consequences. Another critical step is to develop ethical guidelines and regulations for AI development and deployment. These guidelines should address issues like data privacy, algorithmic bias, and the potential for job displacement. They should also promote responsible AI practices, such as ensuring that AI systems are developed and used in ways that benefit society as a whole. Furthermore, it is crucial to cultivate public understanding and engagement in AI ethics. This includes educating the public about AI technologies, their potential benefits and risks, and the ethical considerations involved. Public awareness and engagement are essential to fostering a society that can effectively navigate the challenges and opportunities presented by AI. Beyond these practical measures, it is important to remember that AI is ultimately a tool that can be used for good or ill. The ethical considerations surrounding AI are not just about technology; they are about the values and principles that guide our society. As we develop and deploy AI, we must ensure that it aligns with our values, promotes human wellbeing, and contributes to a just and equitable future for all. The ethical landscape surrounding AI is constantly evolving as the technology itself progresses. We must remain vigilant, engage in ongoing dialogue, and adapt our ethical frameworks to address the emerging challenges and opportunities. The future of AI depends not only on technological advancement but also on our commitment to responsible development and ethical deployment. We must ensure that AI is a force for good, serving humanity's highest aspirations and shaping a future where technology and ethics coexist harmoniously.

Future Prospects of AI

The future of AI is brimming with possibilities, promising a world where technology seamlessly integrates into our lives, revolutionizing every aspect of our existence. As AI continues to evolve, its potential impact on society is immense, raising both exciting opportunities and complex challenges. One of the most significant potential developments in AI is the emergence of artificial general intelligence (AGI). Unlike today's AI systems, which are designed for specific tasks, AGI aims to create machines with human-level intelligence capable of learning, adapting, and solving problems across a wide range of domains. The realization of AGI could lead to ground breaking advancements in various fields, from scientific discovery to creative expression. Imagine AI systems that can design innovative drugs, compose breathtaking symphonies, or even write compelling novels. However, the development of AGI raises profound ethical concerns. If machines surpass human intelligence, what are the implications for our societal structures, our values, and our very existence? Who controls these super-intelligent systems, and how do we ensure they align with human values? These questions are critical to address as we navigate the uncharted territory of AGI. Beyond AGI, AI is poised to transform numerous sectors, leading to a wave of automation that will reshape the global workforce. As AI takes over repetitive and dangerous tasks, some jobs will be displaced, while new opportunities will emerge in fields related to AI development, maintenance, and ethical oversight. The challenge will lie in ensuring that the benefits of AI-driven automation are shared equitably, and that workers are equipped with the skills needed to thrive in the future job market. AI will also play a crucial role in tackling global challenges such as climate change and disease. AI powered tools can analyze vast amounts of data to identify patterns and predict environmental changes, enabling us to develop more sustainable energy solutions and mitigate the impacts of climate change. In healthcare, AI can assist in early disease diagnosis, personalized treatment plans, and the development of novel therapies. However, the use of AI in these sensitive areas raises concerns about data privacy and security. As AI relies on massive datasets, protecting individual privacy and preventing the misuse of data becomes paramount. Robust safeguards are essential to ensure that AI systems are used responsibly and ethically. Another key area of future development is the intersection of AI and human augmentation. Imagine AI powered implants that enhance our cognitive abilities, prosthetic limbs that function seamlessly with the human nervous system, or even virtual reality experiences that blur the lines between reality and simulation. These advancements could revolutionize human capabilities, but also raise ethical questions about what it means to be human and the potential for inequality if these technologies are not accessible to all. Looking ahead, the future of AI holds immense promise for shaping a better world. However, navigating this exciting and uncharted territory requires careful consideration of the ethical, societal, and economic implications. It is crucial to develop responsible AI frameworks that ensure equitable access, mitigate risks, and align with human values. By approaching the development and deployment of AI with wisdom and foresight, we can harness its power for the benefit of all humanity. AI and the Future of Work: The impact of AI on the future of work is a complex and multifaceted topic, generating both excitement and anxiety. While AI is expected to automate many tasks, it is also creating new jobs and transforming existing ones. Job Displacement and Re-skilling: AI-powered automation is likely to displace workers in certain sectors, particularly those involving repetitive tasks. This trend has already been observed in industries like manufacturing, transportation, and customer service. However, it is crucial to remember that technological advancements have always led to job displacement, followed by the emergence of new opportunities. The key to navigating this transition lies in re-skilling and upskilling the workforce. Educational institutions, governments, and companies need to invest in programs that equip workers with the skills needed for the AI-driven economy. This might involve training in AI-related fields, such as data science, machine learning, and software engineering, or in complementary areas like critical thinking, creativity, and complex problem-solving. The Rise of New Jobs: While some jobs will be displaced, AI is also creating new roles in fields such as AI development, data analysis, AI ethics, and AI implementation. These roles will require specialized skills and knowledge, and those who can adapt and acquire these skills will be in high demand. The Future of Human-Machine Collaboration: The future of work is likely to involve a greater degree of collaboration between humans and AI systems. AI can handle routine tasks, freeing up humans to focus on more creative, strategic, and complex problem-solving. This symbiotic relationship can lead to increased productivity, innovation, and efficiency. Ethical Considerations in the

Workplace: As AI becomes more prevalent in the workplace, ethical considerations become paramount. Ensuring fair treatment of workers, preventing algorithmic bias, and addressing issues of data privacy are crucial. Transparency in AI decision making and the right to challenge automated decisions are also essential. AI and Education: AI has the potential to revolutionize education by personalizing learning experiences, providing personalized tutoring, and automating administrative tasks. AI-powered educational tools can analyze student data, identify learning gaps, and provide individualized feedback and support. AI and Healthcare: AI is transforming healthcare in numerous ways, from disease diagnosis and drug discovery to patient care and medical imaging. AI-powered systems can analyze medical records, identify patterns, and predict patient outcomes, leading to more effective diagnoses and treatments. AI in Personalized Medicine: AI is enabling the development of personalized medicine, tailored to individual patients' genetic makeup and specific needs. AI algorithms can analyze vast amounts of data, including genomic information, lifestyle factors, and medical history, to predict disease risk and develop personalized treatment plans. AI in Drug Discovery and Development: AI is accelerating the process of drug discovery by analyzing vast amounts of data to identify potential drug candidates and optimize their design. AI-powered tools are also being used to simulate drug interactions, predict clinical trial outcomes, and accelerate the approval process. AI and the Environment: AI can play a crucial role in addressing environmental challenges such as climate change and pollution. AI powered tools can analyze climate data, predict environmental changes, and optimize energy consumption. AI in Renewable Energy: AI is being used to improve the efficiency and effectiveness of renewable energy sources, such as solar and wind power. AI algorithms can optimize the operation of solar panels and wind turbines, reducing energy costs and maximizing energy output. AI in Environmental Monitoring: AI-powered systems can monitor environmental conditions, detect pollution, and predict natural disasters. AI can analyze satellite imagery, sensor data, and weather patterns to provide real-time information and support decision-making in environmental protection and disaster response.

AI and Transportation: AI is transforming the transportation industry through the development of autonomous vehicles, traffic optimization systems, and personalized mobility solutions. Autonomous Vehicles: AI-powered autonomous vehicles are expected to revolutionize transportation by improving safety, reducing congestion, and optimizing fuel efficiency. Self-driving cars and trucks are already undergoing testing and are expected to become more prevalent in the coming years. Traffic Optimization: AI algorithms can analyze real-time traffic data, identify bottlenecks, and adjust traffic signals to optimize traffic flow, reducing congestion and improving commutes. Personalized Mobility: AI-powered ride-sharing services and public transportation systems can provide personalized mobility solutions, tailoring routes and schedules to individual preferences and needs. AI and Entertainment: AI is transforming the entertainment industry by personalizing content recommendations, creating immersive experiences, and generating new forms of entertainment. Personalized Content Recommendations: AI algorithms are used by streaming services like Netflix and Spotify to analyze user preferences and provide personalized content recommendations, enhancing user engagement and satisfaction. Immersive Entertainment Experiences: AI is being used to create more immersive and interactive entertainment experiences, such as virtual reality games and virtual concerts. AI-Generated Content: AI is capable of generating creative content, such as music, paintings, and even stories. These AI-generated works are pushing the boundaries of artistic expression and raising questions about the nature of creativity and originality. AI and the Future of Humanity: The future of AI is closely intertwined with the future of humanity. As AI continues to evolve, it will have a profound impact on our lives, our work, and our society. The Future of Work and the Rise of the Gig Economy: AI is likely to lead to a more flexible and decentralized workforce, with a greater reliance on the gig economy and freelance work. AI-powered platforms can match workers with tasks, manage schedules, and streamline payments, making it easier for individuals to find work and for businesses to find talent. The Future of Education and Lifelong Learning: AI will play a crucial role in reshaping education, making learning more personalized, accessible, and engaging. AI powered tutors can provide customized instruction, adaptive learning platforms can track student progress, and AI powered tools can automate administrative tasks. The Future of Healthcare and Personalized Medicine: AI is poised to revolutionize healthcare, leading to more accurate diagnoses, personalized treatments, and improved patient outcomes. AI-powered tools can analyze medical records, identify patterns, and predict disease risk, enabling early intervention and more effective treatment plans. The Future of Transportation and Sustainable Mobility: AI is driving the development of autonomous vehicles, smart traffic management systems, and personalized mobility solutions, leading to safer, more efficient, and more sustainable transportation systems. The Future of Entertainment and Creative Expression: AI is transforming the entertainment industry, enhancing user experiences, generating new forms of entertainment, and pushing the boundaries of creative expression. The Future of Ethics and AI Governance: As AI becomes more powerful and pervasive, it is essential to develop ethical frameworks and governance mechanisms to ensure its responsible use. AI governance should address issues such as bias, privacy, security, and transparency. The Future of Human-Machine Collaboration: AI is not intended to replace humans but to augment our abilities, enhancing our productivity and creativity. The future of work will likely involve a greater degree of collaboration between humans and AI systems, leading to new opportunities and challenges. Conclusion: The future of AI is filled with both opportunities and challenges. It has the potential to revolutionize our lives, solve global problems, and enhance our human capabilities. However, it is crucial to approach AI development and deployment with wisdom, ethical considerations, and a focus on creating a more equitable and sustainable future for all. By harnessing the power of AI responsibly, we can create a world where technology empowers humanity and contributes to a brighter future.

Chapter Two
Quantum Computing Revolution

Introduction to Quantum Computing

Imagine a computer that operates not with the familiar bits of 0s and 1s, but with the bizarre and mind-bending rules of quantum mechanics. This is the world of quantum computing, a technology that promises to revolutionize fields ranging from medicine and materials science to cryptography and artificial intelligence. To grasp the power of quantum computing, we must first dive into the strange and wonderful world of quantum mechanics. Unlike classical physics, which governs the everyday objects we see around us, quantum mechanics operates on the scale of atoms and subatomic particles. In this realm, the rules of logic we are accustomed to break down, replaced by a different set of principles. One of the fundamental concepts in quantum mechanics is superposition, the ability of a quantum particle to exist in multiple states simultaneously. Imagine a coin spinning in the air. In classical physics, the coin is either heads or tails, but in quantum mechanics, it can be both heads and tails at the same time until we observe it. This "both-at-once" state is key to quantum computing, as it allows qubits, the quantum equivalent of bits, to hold more information than their classical counterparts. Another fascinating aspect of quantum mechanics is entanglement. Entangled particles, even when separated by vast distances, are linked in a way that defies classical physics. When you measure the state of one entangled particle, you instantly know the state of the other, no matter how far apart they are. This seemingly spooky connection, described by Einstein as "spooky action at a distance," is another crucial element in quantum computing. The power of quantum computing lies in harnessing these quantum phenomena to perform calculations in ways impossible for classical computers. Classical computers process information bit by bit, representing each bit as either a 0 or a 1. Quantum computers, however, use qubits, which can exist in a superposition of states, representing both 0 and 1 simultaneously. This allows them to handle significantly more complex problems. Imagine trying to find a specific grain of sand on a vast beach. A classical computer would have to sift through each grain one by one, a slow and laborious process. A quantum computer, on the other hand, could explore all the grains simultaneously, thanks to the power of superposition. This remarkable capability unlocks potential for solving problems that are currently intractable for classical computers. The applications of quantum computing are vast and varied. In medicine, it could help develop new drugs and therapies by simulating complex biological processes with unprecedented accuracy. It could revolutionize materials science by designing new materials with incredible properties, leading to breakthroughs in energy storage, electronics, and more. Cryptography, the science of secure communication, stands to be significantly impacted by quantum computing. Existing encryption methods, which rely on the difficulty of factoring large numbers, could be easily cracked by a powerful quantum computer. This poses a serious challenge to cybersecurity, but it also opens up new opportunities for developing unbreakable encryption algorithms. However, the road to realizing the full potential of quantum computing is paved with significant challenges. Building and maintaining quantum computers is incredibly complex and expensive. Qubits are extremely fragile and prone to errors, requiring sophisticated techniques for error correction. Despite these hurdles, progress in quantum computing is accelerating rapidly. Companies and research institutions worldwide are pouring resources into developing this revolutionary technology. As we continue to push the boundaries of quantum physics and engineering, we are getting closer to unlocking the immense power of quantum computers. The future of quantum computing holds immense promise, with the potential to reshape our world in ways we can only begin to imagine. While it is still in its early stages of development, the rapid advancements in this field suggest that the quantum revolution may be closer than we think. From the depths of the subatomic realm, quantum computing is poised to transform our world, pushing the limits of computation and revealing new possibilities in science, technology, and beyond.

Qubits and Entanglement

Let's delve into the fascinating realm of quantum computing, a realm where the laws of the microscopic world are harnessed to perform computations in ways unimaginable with traditional computers. The fundamental building block of this revolutionary technology is the qubit. Imagine a coin spinning in the air, its fate uncertain until it lands. This is analogous to a qubit's state. Unlike a conventional bit, which can be either 0 or 1, a qubit exists in a state of superposition, simultaneously representing both 0 and 1. This peculiar quantum property allows qubits to hold far more information than their classical counterparts. To truly grasp the power of quantum computing, we must understand entanglement. Imagine two coins, seemingly independent, yet linked by an invisible thread. When one coin lands heads up, the other instantly flips to tails, no matter the distance between them. This uncanny connection is entanglement. Two entangled qubits share a unified destiny; their fates are intertwined, regardless of physical separation. When one entangled qubit is measured, its partner's state is instantaneously determined, even if they are light years apart. This peculiar phenomenon is known as quantum nonlocality and has profound implications for communication, cryptography, and our understanding of reality itself. Think of entanglement as a symphony of interconnected instruments. Each instrument (qubit) plays its unique note, but the true beauty lies in the harmonious interplay between them. These entangled qubits form a complex quantum orchestra, their combined power exceeding the sum of their individual parts. The potential applications of entanglement in quantum computing are astounding. For example, entangled qubits could be used to develop unbreakable encryption algorithms, revolutionize drug discovery by simulating complex molecular interactions, and even lead to breakthroughs in materials science by enabling the design of entirely new materials with unique properties. But entanglement is not just a theoretical concept; it has been experimentally confirmed in laboratories across the globe. Scientists have successfully entangled photons, atoms, and even larger systems, paving the way for practical applications in quantum computing. To better understand the nature of entanglement, let's explore a classic thought experiment known as Schrödinger's cat. In this thought experiment, a cat is placed inside a box with a device that has a 50% chance of releasing a deadly poison. Until the box is opened, the cat's state is uncertain: it is both alive and dead simultaneously. This is akin to the superposition state of a qubit, where it represents both 0 and 1 until it is measured. Now, imagine two boxes, each containing a cat, and these boxes are entangled. If one box is opened and the cat is found to be dead, we instantly know that the other cat is alive, even without opening its box. This is the essence of entanglement: the fate of one system is instantly linked to the fate of another, regardless of their separation. The implications of this mind-bending phenomenon are far reaching. Entanglement offers a way to break through the limitations of classical computing, enabling the development of powerful algorithms capable of solving problems that are currently intractable. For example, quantum computers could be used to break the encryption algorithms that protect our digital information, raising concerns about the security of our online world. However, entanglement also presents a tantalizing opportunity to create new encryption methods that are unbreakable, even by quantum computers. This revolutionary technology could potentially usher in a new era of secure communication and data protection. The world of quantum computing is still in its early stages, but its potential impact on our lives is undeniable. By harnessing the power of qubits and entanglement, we are entering a new era of computation that promises to transform the way we live, work, and interact with the world. As we venture deeper into this fascinating realm, we will explore the remarkable applications of quantum computing in medicine, materials science, and cryptography. We will also delve into the challenges that lie ahead, the limitations of current quantum computers, and the ongoing race to develop more powerful and stable quantum systems. So, buckle up and prepare for an exhilarating journey into the quantum world, where the laws of physics bend and the possibilities seem limitless.

Applications in Medicine and Cryptography

The realm of medicine, with its intricate complexities and ever-evolving landscape, stands poised to be profoundly transformed by the emergence of quantum computing. This revolutionary technology, with its unparalleled computational power, holds the potential to revolutionize drug discovery, diagnostics, and personalized therapies, ushering in a new era of precision medicine. Imagine a world where diseases are diagnosed with unprecedented accuracy, treatments are tailored to individual genetic profiles, and new drugs are developed at an astonishing pace. This is the future that quantum computing promises to bring. At the heart of this transformation lies the ability of quantum computers to tackle problems that are intractable for classical computers. These problems, often involving vast and complex data sets, are fundamental to many aspects of medical research and practice. Quantum Computing's Impact on Drug Discovery Drug discovery, a lengthy and costly process, relies heavily on computational modelling and simulation. Traditional methods, however, are often limited in their ability to accurately simulate the intricate interactions of molecules within the human body. Quantum computers, with their ability to manipulate quantum states, could revolutionize this process by enabling scientists to model these interactions with unparalleled fidelity. By simulating the behaviour of molecules at the atomic level, quantum computers could help researchers design new drugs that are more effective, have fewer side effects, and are tailored to individual patients. This ability to simulate complex biological processes could also accelerate the development of personalized therapies, enabling doctors to predict the efficacy of different treatments for specific patients based on their genetic makeup. For example, researchers at pharmaceutical giant Roche have already begun using quantum computers to study protein folding, a crucial aspect of drug discovery. Protein folding refers to the complex process by which proteins fold into their three-dimensional structures, which are essential for their biological function. This process is notoriously difficult to simulate with classical computers, but quantum computers have shown promise in tackling this challenge. By understanding the intricate interplay of forces that govern protein folding, researchers can develop new drugs that target specific proteins involved in disease processes. The ability to simulate protein folding with high accuracy could also lead to the development of new diagnostics that can detect disease markers at an early stage, allowing for timely intervention and improving patient outcomes. Quantum Computing in Diagnostics and Imaging Quantum computers can also transform medical diagnostics and imaging, providing doctors with a more comprehensive and accurate view of their patients' health. One promising application of quantum computing in diagnostics is the development of quantum sensors. These sensors, based on principles of quantum mechanics, can detect minute variations in magnetic fields, electric fields, and other physical quantities, surpassing the capabilities of conventional sensors. This enhanced sensitivity could revolutionize magnetic resonance imaging (MRI), a technique used to visualize internal organs and tissues. By leveraging the power of quantum sensors, MRI scans could provide much clearer and more detailed images, enabling doctors to detect abnormalities and diseases at an earlier stage. Quantum computers could also play a vital role in developing new diagnostic tests that are faster, more accurate, and more sensitive than existing methods. For instance, researchers are exploring the use of quantum computers to develop highly specific and sensitive tests for detecting the presence of cancer cells in blood samples, a process that could lead to earlier diagnosis and more effective treatment. Moreover, quantum computing could empower doctors to perform real-time analysis of patient data, enabling them to make more informed decisions about treatment plans. By analyzing vast amounts of data from electronic health records, medical imaging, and genetic tests, quantum computers could provide insights into individual patient characteristics and predict how they might respond to different therapies. The Promise of Personalized Medicine Personalized medicine, an approach that tailors medical treatments to individual patients, is rapidly gaining momentum. Quantum computing can play a pivotal role in this revolution by enabling the development of more targeted and effective therapies. Quantum computers can help researchers identify individuals at risk for specific diseases based on their genetic makeup. By analyzing large datasets of genetic information, these computers can identify genetic variations that may predispose individuals to certain diseases. This knowledge could lead to the development of preventative measures and personalized interventions to reduce the risk of disease development. Quantum computers can also help personalize cancer treatments by providing insights into the unique characteristics of individual tumours. By analyzing genomic data from tumour cells, quantum computers can identify specific mutations that drive tumour growth. This information can then be used to select the most effective chemotherapy drugs or immunotherapy therapies for each patient. Quantum Computing and Cryptographic Security While the potential of quantum computing to revolutionize medicine is remarkable, its impact extends far beyond healthcare. The same principles that enable these medical breakthroughs could also revolutionize cybersecurity and cryptography. Cryptography, the art of secure communication, relies heavily on mathematical algorithms that are difficult to break with classical computers. However, the advent of quantum computers poses a significant challenge to these traditional cryptographic methods. Quantum computers can efficiently crack some of the most widely used encryption algorithms, rendering them vulnerable to attack. This threat has spurred a rapid shift towards the development of quantum-resistant cryptography, which aims to create encryption algorithms that are secure even against the computational power of quantum computers. One promising approach is based on the concept of lattice based cryptography, which relies on the complexity of mathematical problems related to lattices, multidimensional geometric structures. Lattice-based cryptography has shown resilience against attacks from quantum computers and is considered a strong candidate for future encryption systems. The development of quantum-resistant cryptography is crucial for protecting sensitive information in a world where quantum computers are becoming more readily available. It will be essential for safeguarding financial transactions, online communications, and other sensitive data from potential attacks.

Challenges and the Future of Quantum Computing

Despite the vast potential of quantum computing, there are still significant challenges that need to be overcome before it can be fully realized. These challenges include: Scaling up quantum computers: Building large-scale quantum computers with sufficient qubits to tackle complex problems is a major engineering feat. Current quantum computers are still relatively small and prone to errors. Developing robust error correction methods: Quantum systems are highly sensitive to noise and decoherence, which can introduce errors into calculations. Developing robust error correction methods is crucial for ensuring the reliability of quantum computers. Bridging the gap between theory and practice: Developing algorithms specifically designed for quantum computers is essential for leveraging their unique computational capabilities. Despite these challenges, the field of quantum computing is rapidly advancing. Researchers are making significant progress in overcoming these hurdles, paving the way for the widespread adoption of this transformative technology. The future of quantum computing is bright, with the potential to reshape industries, solve intractable problems, and create new possibilities. In the realm of medicine, quantum computing promises to revolutionize drug discovery, diagnostics, and personalized therapies, leading to more effective treatments and improved patient outcomes. In the digital age, quantum computing will reshape cybersecurity and cryptography, ensuring the security of our digital world. As we continue to push the boundaries of technological innovation, quantum computing stands poised to usher in a new era of scientific discovery and technological advancement, profoundly impacting our lives in ways we can only begin to imagine. Current Challenges and Developments While quantum computers hold immense promise, their development faces significant technical hurdles. Building a quantum computer is akin to constructing a delicate, complex machine, requiring meticulous control over its environment and components. One major challenge lies in maintaining the coherence of qubits, the building blocks of quantum information. Qubits are notoriously fragile, easily disrupted by noise and interference from their surroundings. This fragility makes it incredibly difficult to maintain their quantum states, crucial for performing quantum operations. Researchers are employing various strategies to address this challenge, including shielding qubits from environmental disturbances using specialized materials and cooling them to extremely low temperatures, often near absolute zero. These methods help to minimize decoherence, the loss of quantum information due to interactions with the environment. Another significant hurdle is scaling up quantum computers. Current quantum computers are still relatively small, limited to a few dozen or hundreds of qubits. To unlock the full potential of quantum computing for tackling complex problems, we need to build machines with millions or even billions of qubits. Scaling up quantum systems is a complex engineering feat, demanding advances in qubit fabrication, control systems, and error correction techniques. Despite these challenges, there have been remarkable breakthroughs in recent years. Researchers have demonstrated the ability to control qubits with increasing precision and perform complex quantum algorithms. Several companies are investing heavily in quantum computing research, developing different types of quantum computers based on various technologies, including superconducting qubits, trapped ions, and photonic qubits. The race to build the first fault-tolerant quantum computer is heating up, with several research groups on the cusp of major advancements. A fault-tolerant quantum computer would be able to correct errors that inevitably occur in quantum systems, paving the way for large-scale, practical quantum applications. The field of quantum computing is rapidly evolving, with new breakthroughs and discoveries emerging regularly. Recent research has yielded promising advancements in qubit control, error correction, and scaling. For example, scientists have achieved record-breaking levels of coherence in superconducting qubits, demonstrating the ability to maintain their quantum states for extended periods. These advances suggest that the path towards building practical, large-scale quantum computers is becoming clearer. Beyond the realm of individual qubits, researchers are making progress in developing techniques to entangle multiple qubits. Entanglement, a fundamental principle of quantum mechanics, allows for the creation of highly correlated states, essential for performing quantum computations. This progress is crucial for enabling the development of more complex quantum algorithms and solving a wider range of problems. While quantum computing technology is still in its infancy, the potential benefits are vast and far-reaching. Its impact could be felt in various fields, including medicine, materials science, finance, and cryptography. For instance, quantum computers could revolutionize drug discovery by simulating the behaviour of molecules at a quantum level, allowing scientists to design new drugs more efficiently and effectively. In materials science, quantum computers could be used to design novel materials with tailored properties, leading to advancements in areas like energy storage, electronics, and aerospace. The financial industry could also benefit from quantum computing, as it can be used to optimize investment strategies and manage financial risk. Quantum computing could also have profound implications for cryptography. Current encryption algorithms rely on the difficulty of factoring large numbers, a task that is computationally challenging for classical computers but could be efficiently solved by a quantum computer. This poses a significant threat to current encryption schemes, motivating the development of new, quantum-resistant algorithms. The development of quantum computing is a global endeavour, with researchers and companies around the world working to push the boundaries of this emerging technology. International collaborations and partnerships are essential for accelerating progress in this field. As we continue to advance our understanding of quantum mechanics and develop new technological solutions, the future of quantum computing holds immense potential to transform our world. To fully appreciate the potential of quantum computing, it's crucial to understand its core principles. Quantum mechanics, the theory governing the behaviour of matter at the atomic and subatomic levels, introduces concepts that differ significantly from our everyday experience. Unlike classical bits, which can represent either 0 or 1, qubits can exist in a superposition of states, simultaneously representing both 0 and 1. This quantum property allows for the storage and manipulation of exponentially more information than classical bits. Entanglement is another key concept in quantum computing. It describes a phenomenon where two or more qubits become inextricably linked, even when physically separated. The state of one entangled qubit instantly influences the state of the others, regardless of the distance between them. This remarkable property allows for the execution of quantum operations on multiple qubits simultaneously, leading to significant speedups for certain computations. Quantum algorithms leverage these unique quantum properties to perform calculations in a fundamentally different way than classical algorithms. Some quantum algorithms have been shown to solve problems exponentially faster than their classical counterparts, making them ideal for tasks that are currently intractable for classical computers. For example, Shor's algorithm is a quantum algorithm that can efficiently factor large numbers, posing a threat to modern cryptographic systems. Other quantum algorithms, like Grover's algorithm, can accelerate searching through unstructured databases, making them valuable for applications in areas like data mining and machine learning. While the development of quantum computing is still in its early stages, the potential benefits for science, medicine, finance, and cryptography are undeniable. As the field continues to progress, we can expect to see more breakthroughs, faster algorithms, and increasingly powerful quantum computers. The future of quantum computing is bright, holding the promise of revolutionizing our world in ways we can only begin to imagine. Future of Quantum Computing The future of quantum computing is brimming with possibilities, holding the potential to reshape our world in profound ways. It's a field that's still in its nascent stages, but the rapid advancements being made suggest that we're on the cusp of a quantum revolution. Imagine a world where drug discovery is accelerated, materials science is transformed, and cryptography becomes virtually unbreakable—this is the promise of quantum computing. While current quantum computers are still relatively small and prone to errors, researchers are steadily making progress in overcoming these challenges. The race to build larger and more stable quantum computers is heating up, with companies like Google, IBM, and Microsoft vying for the lead. The development of error correction techniques is crucial to improving the reliability of quantum computers, paving the way for their widespread adoption. One of the most exciting applications of quantum computing lies in the realm of medicine. Quantum algorithms could revolutionize drug discovery by enabling scientists to simulate the complex interactions of molecules with unprecedented accuracy. This could lead to the development of new drugs and therapies that are more effective and have fewer side effects. The power of quantum computers extends to materials science as well. Quantum simulations could unlock the secrets of new materials with tailored properties, potentially leading to the creation of superconductors, advanced batteries, and revolutionary solar cells. These breakthroughs could have a profound impact on energy production, storage, and transportation. In the realm of cryptography, quantum computing poses both a threat and an opportunity. While quantum computers could break existing encryption algorithms, they also offer the potential for new, more secure cryptographic methods. This area of research is crucial for safeguarding sensitive data in a world increasingly reliant on digital technologies. As quantum computers become more powerful and accessible, they will likely impact various industries, from finance and logistics to artificial intelligence and machine learning. Quantum machine learning could lead to the development of AI systems that are more powerful and efficient than anything we've seen before. Beyond its practical applications, quantum computing raises philosophical questions about the nature of reality and the limits of computation. It challenges our understanding of how information is processed and stored, opening up new avenues for exploration in physics and computer science. The journey to a quantum future is not without its challenges. Building and operating quantum computers is a complex and costly endeavour. The field faces technical hurdles, including the need for better error correction techniques and the development of new materials that can withstand the extreme conditions required for quantum computation. However, the potential rewards are immense. Quantum computing has the power to transform our world in ways that we can only begin to imagine. It is a field that is rapidly evolving and has the potential to revolutionize medicine, materials science, cryptography, and many other fields. As we look toward the future, it's clear that quantum computing is poised to play a pivotal role in shaping the world around us. It's a technology with the potential to solve some of humanity's most pressing challenges and unlock new frontiers of scientific discovery. The journey is only just beginning, but the potential is boundless. While it's difficult to predict the exact trajectory of quantum computing, it's safe to say that the future holds exciting possibilities. We can expect to see continued advancements in quantum hardware and software, leading to the development of more powerful and reliable quantum computers. These advancements will open up new applications in various fields, revolutionizing industries and impacting our daily lives in profound ways. The future of quantum computing is not just about technological advancements but also about the ethical and societal implications of this powerful technology. As quantum computers become more accessible, it's crucial to consider how they will be used and the potential impact on privacy, security, and the future of work. The ethical considerations surrounding quantum computing are complex and require careful consideration. For instance, the ability to break existing encryption algorithms could have significant implications for data security and privacy. It's essential to develop new cryptographic methods that are resistant to quantum attacks to ensure the confidentiality and integrity of sensitive information. The impact of quantum computing on the job market is another crucial consideration. As quantum computers become more sophisticated, they could automate tasks that are currently performed by humans, potentially leading to job displacement in certain sectors. It's important to address these challenges proactively by investing in education and training programs to prepare the workforce for the jobs of the future. As quantum computing continues to advance, we must engage in open and informed discussions about its potential benefits and risks. It's crucial to ensure that this powerful technology is developed and used responsibly for the betterment of humanity. In conclusion, the future of quantum computing is full of promise and uncertainty. While the technology faces significant challenges, the potential benefits are too great to ignore. The journey to a quantum future will require continued collaboration between scientists, engineers, policymakers, and society as a whole to ensure that this powerful technology is developed and used responsibly for the benefit of all. The next decade will be a pivotal time in the history of quantum computing, and the choices we make today will shape the world of tomorrow.

Chapter Three
Sustainable Energy Innovations

Renewable Energy Sources

The sun, a colossal nuclear reactor in the sky, has been powering life on Earth for billions of years. Now, humanity is harnessing its energy to power our homes, businesses, and even entire cities. Solar energy, a renewable and abundant resource, is rapidly gaining traction as a viable alternative to fossil fuels. Solar panels, like giant leaves absorbing sunlight, convert photons into electrons, generating electricity. This clean energy source is becoming increasingly affordable and efficient, with advancements in photovoltaic technology constantly pushing the boundaries. From rooftop installations to vast solar farms, the sun's energy is being harnessed across the globe, contributing to a cleaner and more sustainable future. But the sun doesn't always shine, and that's where wind power comes in. Harnessing the power of the wind, wind turbines stand tall like silent giants, their blades gracefully rotating in the breeze, generating electricity. Wind energy, another renewable source, is particularly abundant in coastal areas and open plains. The wind's kinetic energy is converted into electricity through sophisticated generators, creating a clean and sustainable source of power. Wind turbines have become a common sight across the world, contributing significantly to reducing our reliance on fossil fuels. The wind and the sun are not the only renewable energy sources we can tap into. The Earth itself possesses a vast reservoir of renewable energy in the form of geothermal power. Deep beneath the surface, the Earth's core generates immense heat, which can be harnessed to produce electricity. Geothermal power plants tap into this heat by drilling deep into the Earth's crust, extracting hot water or steam, and converting it into electricity. This source of energy is particularly stable and reliable, providing a continuous flow of clean power, regardless of weather conditions. Hydropower, the oldest and most mature renewable energy source, harnesses the power of flowing water to generate electricity. Dams built across rivers create reservoirs, and the water's potential energy is converted into electricity as it flows through turbines. Hydropower is a significant contributor to global energy production, offering a reliable and sustainable source of power. However, large-scale dam construction can have environmental impacts, such as disrupting ecosystems and affecting water flow. Beyond these established renewable energy sources, new technologies are emerging, promising to further revolutionize our energy landscape. Bioenergy, derived from organic matter like wood, crops, and waste, offers a carbon neutral alternative to fossil fuels. Biomass power plants burn organic materials to generate electricity, while biofuels produced from plant oils and other organic sources can power vehicles. Bioenergy is a promising renewable resource, particularly in regions with abundant agricultural resources and waste products. Hydrogen fuel cells, often hailed as the future of clean energy, offer a unique and versatile solution. These cells convert hydrogen gas into electricity through a chemical reaction, producing only water as a by-product. Hydrogen can be produced from various sources, including water electrolysis using renewable energy. The prospect of a hydrogen economy, powered by clean and efficient fuel cells, holds significant promise for reducing our reliance on fossil fuels and achieving a truly sustainable future. The integration of renewable energy sources into existing power grids is a complex and challenging undertaking. Renewable energy sources are intermittent, meaning their output can fluctuate depending on weather conditions. Solar power, for instance, is only available during daylight hours, while wind power relies on consistent wind speeds. Integrating these variable sources into the grid requires sophisticated energy storage solutions to ensure a stable and reliable power supply. Battery technology is rapidly advancing, offering a promising solution for storing renewable energy. Lithium ion batteries, commonly used in electric vehicles and smartphones, are becoming increasingly efficient and cost effective. Other energy storage solutions, such as pumped hydro storage, compressed air energy storage, and flow batteries, are also being developed and deployed. These technologies play a crucial role in ensuring the reliability of renewable energy systems, enabling us to store excess energy generated during periods of high wind and sunshine for use when demand is high or renewables are not available. The future of energy consumption is intertwined with the development of smart grids and energy management systems. Smart grids, incorporating advanced technologies like sensors, communication networks, and data analytics, enable real-time monitoring and control of energy flow. These systems optimize energy efficiency, reduce waste, and integrate renewable energy sources seamlessly. By connecting energy consumers and producers through a network of smart devices, smart grids empower individuals to actively manage their energy consumption, potentially leading to significant reductions in overall energy demand. The transition to a renewable energy future is not without its challenges. The initial cost of renewable energy technologies can be high, and the development of large-scale renewable energy infrastructure requires significant investments. Furthermore, the manufacturing and deployment of renewable energy technologies involve complex supply chains and resource dependencies, requiring careful consideration of environmental and social impacts. Despite these challenges, the global movement toward renewable energy is gaining momentum. Governments, businesses, and individuals are increasingly investing in and adopting renewable energy technologies, driven by environmental concerns, economic opportunities, and a desire for a more sustainable future. The shift towards renewable energy sources represents a paradigm shift in our relationship with the planet, moving away from finite fossil fuels towards an infinite supply of clean and sustainable energy from the sun, wind, and Earth's resources. The future of energy is bright with the promise of a clean, sustainable, and resilient energy system. As we continue to innovate and develop new technologies, renewable energy will play an increasingly critical role in powering our planet, ensuring a brighter future for generations to come.

The Promise of Hydrogen Fuel Cells

The promise of hydrogen fuel cells lies in their ability to produce clean electricity without any emissions, offering a potential solution to our dependence on fossil fuels. Hydrogen fuel cells operate on a simple yet ingenious principle: they convert hydrogen gas into electricity through a chemical reaction. This reaction involves the splitting of hydrogen molecules into protons and electrons, with the protons passing through a membrane and the electrons flowing through an external circuit, generating an electric current. Imagine this process as a miniature power plant within a fuel cell, quietly and efficiently producing electricity. Unlike traditional combustion engines that burn fuel to release energy, hydrogen fuel cells use a chemical process that doesn't produce harmful by-products like greenhouse gases. The core of a hydrogen fuel cell is a stack of membranes, known as electrolytes, sandwiched between two electrodes. Hydrogen gas is fed into the anode, the negative electrode, where it encounters a catalyst, typically platinum. This catalyst breaks down the hydrogen molecules into protons and electrons. The protons then travel through the electrolyte membrane to the cathode, the positive electrode. Meanwhile, the electrons are forced to flow through an external circuit, creating an electric current. At the cathode, the electrons combine with the protons and oxygen from the air to form water, the only by-product of the reaction. This process, called electrolysis, essentially reverses the process of water decomposition, yielding electricity and water as the only output. While the concept might seem straightforward, the technology behind hydrogen fuel cells involves intricate engineering and material science advancements. To optimize the process, scientists and engineers have been exploring different types of electrolytes, catalysts, and electrode materials. One of the key challenges in making hydrogen fuel cells more viable is finding efficient and cost-effective ways to produce hydrogen. While hydrogen is the most abundant element in the universe, it doesn't exist in its pure form on Earth. It needs to be extracted from other sources like water or fossil fuels. Electrolysis, a process similar to that happening within the fuel cell, can be used to extract hydrogen from water. However, this process requires significant energy input, raising concerns about its environmental impact. Research is ongoing to develop more efficient and sustainable methods for producing hydrogen, including using renewable energy sources like solar or wind power to drive electrolysis. Another major challenge is the storage and transportation of hydrogen. Due to its low density, hydrogen needs to be compressed or liquefied to store and transport effectively. This adds complexity and cost to the overall system. Finding safer and more efficient ways to store and transport hydrogen remains a critical aspect of its widespread adoption. Despite these challenges, hydrogen fuel cells hold tremendous promise for various applications. They are particularly well-suited for powering vehicles, as they can be integrated into existing car infrastructure. Electric vehicles powered by hydrogen fuel cells offer several advantages over traditional gasoline-powered vehicles. They are significantly cleaner, emitting only water vapour, and they have a longer range than battery-powered electric vehicles. Beyond transportation, hydrogen fuel cells find applications in various industries. They can power backup generators for homes and businesses, providing a reliable source of electricity during power outages. In the energy sector, hydrogen fuel cells can be used to generate electricity in remote locations or where grid connections are limited. They can also be used to power portable devices like laptops and smartphones. Furthermore, hydrogen fuel cells can be used in conjunction with renewable energy sources to create a more robust energy system. By storing excess energy from solar or wind power, hydrogen fuel cells can help balance the intermittent nature of these renewable sources. This creates a more reliable and sustainable energy grid. The future of hydrogen fuel cells looks bright, with ongoing research and development leading to significant advancements in efficiency and cost-effectiveness. As the world continues to grapple with climate change and the need for clean energy sources, hydrogen fuel cells are emerging as a promising solution for a more sustainable future. Here's a closer look at some of the key areas where hydrogen fuel cells are poised to make a significant impact:

1. Transportation: The automotive industry is leading the charge in adopting hydrogen fuel cell technology. Companies like Toyota, Hyundai, and Honda have already introduced hydrogen fuel cell vehicles (FCVs) to the market. These vehicles offer several advantages over conventional gasoline-powered cars. They produce zero tailpipe emissions, have a longer range than battery electric vehicles (BEVs), and can be refuelled quickly. One of the key benefits of FCVs is their ability to refuel in just a few minutes, similar to gasoline-powered vehicles. This is a significant advantage over BEVs, which typically require several hours to charge. While the infrastructure for hydrogen refuelling stations is still developing, several countries, including Japan, South Korea, and Germany, are investing in building a robust network of fuelling stations. Beyond passenger cars, hydrogen fuel cells are also being explored for other transportation applications, including buses, trucks, and trains. In 2014, Toyota unveiled a hydrogen fuel cell bus, and several cities around the world are now using these buses in public transportation. The use of hydrogen fuel cells in heavy-duty trucks is also gaining traction, with companies like Hyundai and Daimler leading the way in developing these vehicles. The potential of hydrogen fuel cells in transportation is not limited to land-based vehicles. Companies like Ballard Power Systems are developing hydrogen fuel cell systems for marine applications, including ferries, tugboats, and even cargo ships. The use of hydrogen fuel cells in maritime transportation could significantly reduce emissions from shipping, which is currently a major contributor to air pollution.

2. Power Generation: Hydrogen fuel cells are finding increasing applications in power generation, particularly in distributed generation systems and off-grid applications. They offer a clean and efficient way to produce electricity without the need for fossil fuels. One key advantage of hydrogen fuel cells for power generation is their ability to provide continuous power, unlike solar or wind power, which are intermittent sources. This makes them ideal for backup power systems in homes, businesses, and critical infrastructure. In the event of a power outage, hydrogen fuel cells can provide reliable electricity, ensuring the continued operation of essential services. Hydrogen fuel cells are also well-suited for powering remote communities and locations that lack access to the electricity grid. They can be used to generate electricity in rural areas, disaster relief zones, or remote military installations. This makes them particularly important in areas where grid connections are costly or impossible. In addition to providing standalone power generation, hydrogen fuel cells can be integrated into the existing electricity grid to provide grid stabilization and enhance the reliability of renewable energy sources. They can act as energy storage devices, absorbing excess energy from solar or wind power and releasing it back into the grid when demand is high.

3. Portable Power: Hydrogen fuel cells are also emerging as a viable option for powering portable devices like laptops, smartphones, and drones. Their high energy density and clean operation make them ideal for applications where space and weight are limited. Unlike batteries, which need to be recharged periodically, hydrogen fuel cells can provide continuous power for extended periods. This makes them particularly well-suited for applications where access to electricity is limited or unreliable, such as camping, hiking, or remote work. In addition to powering consumer devices, hydrogen fuel cells are also finding applications in the military and emergency response sectors. They can be used to power portable generators for field operations, communications equipment, and medical devices. Their compact size and lightweight design make them highly portable and adaptable to various environments.

4. Industrial Applications: Hydrogen fuel cells are increasingly being used in industrial settings, where they can provide clean and reliable power for various processes. They are particularly well-suited for applications requiring high power output, such as materials processing, manufacturing, and chemical production. One key advantage of hydrogen fuel cells in industrial applications is their ability to operate at high efficiency and low emissions. They can be used to power forklifts, cranes, and other heavy-duty equipment, reducing reliance on fossil fuels and lowering greenhouse gas emissions. In the chemical industry, hydrogen fuel cells can be used to produce clean hydrogen gas, which can be used as a feedstock for various chemical processes. This can help reduce the carbon footprint of industrial processes and contribute to a more sustainable chemical industry. The use of hydrogen fuel cells in industrial settings is expected to grow significantly in the coming years as companies look for ways to reduce their environmental impact and meet increasing regulations on greenhouse gas emissions.

5. Building Applications: Hydrogen fuel cells are also finding applications in building energy systems, providing clean and efficient power for residential and commercial buildings. They can be used to heat water, provide space heating, and generate electricity, reducing reliance on fossil fuels and lowering energy costs. One key advantage of hydrogen fuel cells in building applications is their ability to integrate seamlessly with existing building infrastructure. They can be installed as stand-alone systems or as part of a hybrid system that combines renewable energy sources and energy storage. Hydrogen fuel cells can also be used to power building-scale energy storage systems, providing a clean and efficient way to store excess energy from solar or wind power. This allows buildings to reduce their reliance on the electricity grid and achieve greater energy independence. The use of hydrogen fuel cells in buildings is expected to grow as homeowners and businesses seek ways to reduce their energy bills and environmental impact. As the technology becomes more affordable and efficient, hydrogen fuel cells are poised to become a standard part of the building energy landscape. The potential of hydrogen fuel cells extends beyond these specific applications.

Their versatility and clean operation make them a promising solution for various energy challenges, from powering remote communities to supporting the development of a sustainable energy grid. As research and development continue to advance, hydrogen fuel cells are poised to play a crucial role in shaping a cleaner, more sustainable future. In conclusion, hydrogen fuel cells offer a promising avenue for a sustainable energy future, with the potential to transform transportation, power generation, and various industries. However, there are still challenges to overcome, including the cost and efficiency of hydrogen production, storage, and transportation. Continued research and development, along with government support and industry collaboration, are crucial to accelerating the adoption of this clean energy technology and realizing its full potential.

Integrating Renewable Energy into Grids

The transition to a sustainable energy future hinges on our ability to seamlessly integrate renewable energy sources into existing power grids. This is a complex undertaking, demanding a multifaceted approach to overcome the inherent challenges. The core challenge lies in the intermittent nature of renewable energy sources, primarily solar and wind power. The sun doesn't always shine, and the wind doesn't always blow consistently. This variability poses a significant hurdle for grid operators, who need to ensure a continuous and reliable power supply. Imagine a city relying solely on solar energy. During cloudy days or night time, the solar panels would produce little to no electricity, potentially leading to power outages. This highlights the critical need for effective energy storage solutions and grid management strategies to address the intermittent nature of renewables. To bridge this gap, a plethora of technological advancements are being explored and implemented. Energy Storage Solutions: Batteries: Lithium-ion batteries, commonly found in electric vehicles, are rapidly becoming a cornerstone of energy storage. Their ability to store energy efficiently and discharge it quickly makes them ideal for smoothing out fluctuations in renewable energy output. Large-scale battery storage systems are being deployed at power plants and grid level, enabling the storage of excess energy generated during peak production periods and its release when demand exceeds supply. These batteries act as a buffer, ensuring continuous power flow even during periods of low renewable energy generation. Pumped Hydro Storage: A mature and proven technology, pumped hydro storage involves using excess energy to pump water uphill into a reservoir. When energy demand exceeds supply, the stored water is released back downhill, driving turbines to generate electricity. This system boasts high efficiency and long storage duration, making it an attractive option for large-scale grid storage. However, its geographical limitations, requiring suitable terrain with water sources and reservoirs, limit its widespread adoption. Compressed Air Energy Storage (CAES): This method involves compressing air using excess energy, storing it in underground caverns or tanks. When energy is needed, the compressed air is released, driving turbines to generate electricity. CAES offers longer storage durations than batteries and is suitable for large-scale applications. However, its implementation requires significant infrastructure investment, including air compression and storage facilities. Smart Grid Technology: Smart grid technology is revolutionizing the way we manage energy flow. These intelligent grids are equipped with advanced sensors, communication networks, and control systems that enable real-time monitoring and dynamic adjustments to energy production and consumption. Demand Response: Smart grids can leverage demand response programs to incentivize consumers to reduce their energy consumption during peak demand periods. This can be achieved through time-of-use pricing, where electricity is priced higher during peak hours, encouraging consumers to shift their energy usage to off-peak hours. Alternatively, utilities can offer financial incentives for consumers to temporarily reduce their energy usage during critical periods, such as during extreme weather events. Distributed Generation: Smart grids facilitate the integration of distributed generation sources, such as rooftop solar panels and small-scale wind turbines, into the grid. This enables individual households and businesses to generate their own energy and sell surplus electricity back to the grid. Distributed generation not only reduces reliance on centralized power plants but also enhances grid resilience by providing alternative energy sources in case of disruptions. Integration Strategies: Forecasting and Prediction: Advanced forecasting tools, powered by machine learning and weather data analysis, help predict the output of renewable energy sources. This information enables grid operators to proactively adjust energy production and dispatch from other sources to compensate for fluctuations in renewable generation. Flexible Generation: Integrating flexible generation sources, such as natural gas power plants that can ramp up and down quickly, allows grid operators to adjust power output to match fluctuating renewable energy supply. These flexible sources provide a critical back-up for maintaining grid stability. Interconnection and Grid Synchronization: Connecting multiple renewable energy sources and grids across vast geographical areas allows for pooling and sharing resources. When one region experiences a dip in renewable energy output, others can compensate, ensuring a more stable overall energy supply. The Promise of Hydrogen: Hydrogen fuel cells offer a compelling solution for long duration energy storage and grid decarbonisation. These cells convert hydrogen into electricity through a chemical reaction, producing water as a by-product. The potential of hydrogen lies in its ability to store energy from renewable sources, such as wind and solar, for extended periods. This stored energy can be readily accessed to meet energy demand during periods of low renewable energy generation. The integration of hydrogen into the grid involves several key steps: Production: Hydrogen can be produced through electrolysis, using renewable electricity to split water into hydrogen and oxygen. This process is currently expensive but is rapidly becoming more efficient and cost-effective with advancements in electrolyser technology. Storage: Hydrogen can be stored in underground caverns, salt formations, or pressurized tanks, offering a reliable and scalable storage solution. Transportation: Hydrogen can be transported through pipelines, similar to natural gas, or as compressed gas in specialized tankers. Utilization: Hydrogen can be used directly in fuel cells to generate electricity or blended with natural gas to fuel power plants. Additionally, hydrogen can be used in transportation, particularly for heavy-duty vehicles like buses and trucks. Challenges and Opportunities: Despite the significant progress in renewable energy integration, several challenges persist: Cost: The cost of renewable energy technology, particularly for large-scale installations, remains a significant barrier. However, ongoing innovation and economies of scale are gradually reducing costs, making renewable energy increasingly competitive with traditional fossil fuels. Infrastructure: Integrating renewable energy sources into existing grids requires extensive infrastructure upgrades, including new transmission lines, substations, and control systems. This can involve significant investment and regulatory hurdles. Social Acceptance: Public perception and acceptance of renewable energy projects, particularly wind and solar farms, can be a hurdle. Concerns over aesthetics, environmental impacts, and land use can hinder project development. Addressing these concerns through community engagement, transparent communication, and robust environmental impact assessments is crucial for gaining public support. The Future of Renewable Energy Integration: The future of renewable energy integration is bright, with ongoing advancements in technology and policy pushing us toward a more sustainable energy future. Increased Grid Flexibility: Smart grids and energy storage solutions will continue to play a pivotal role in enhancing grid flexibility and reliability, accommodating the intermittent nature of renewable energy sources. Hydrogen Economy: The development of a hydrogen economy, with its potential for long-duration energy storage and decarbonisation, holds immense promise for transitioning to a clean energy future. Decentralized Energy Systems: Distributed generation, facilitated by smart grids, will empower individuals and businesses to become active participants in the energy market, creating a more resilient and localized energy system. As we move towards a sustainable energy future, integrating renewable energy sources into our grids is not just an option but a necessity. By embracing innovation, addressing challenges, and fostering collaboration, we can harness the power of renewable energy to build a more resilient, equitable, and sustainable energy system for generations to come. Technological Advancements in Energy Storage the quest for sustainable energy solutions is one of the most pressing challenges of our time. As we grapple with the consequences of climate change and dwindling fossil fuel reserves, the need for efficient and renewable energy sources has never been more apparent. Fortunately, technological advancements are paving the way for a cleaner and more sustainable energy future, particularly in the realm of energy storage. Energy storage, simply put, is the ability to capture and retain energy generated from various sources for later use. This is crucial for smoothing out the intermittent nature of renewable energy sources like solar and wind power, ensuring a reliable supply even when the sun isn't shining or the wind isn't blowing. One of the most prominent breakthroughs in energy storage is the rapid evolution of battery technology. Lithium-ion batteries, which power everything from smartphones to electric vehicles, have undergone a dramatic transformation in recent years. Their energy density has increased significantly, meaning they can store more energy in a smaller space. This translates to longer-lasting devices and greater range for electric cars. Furthermore, the cost of lithium-ion batteries has plummeted, making them more accessible for a wider range of applications. This has been a game-changer for the renewable energy sector, as it has brought down the cost of storing solar and wind energy. However, lithium-ion batteries aren't without their limitations. Their reliance on finite resources like lithium and cobalt raises concerns about sustainability and potential supply chain disruptions. Moreover, their safety can be compromised in certain situations, leading to fires or explosions. Research and development efforts are addressing these challenges head-on. Scientists and engineers are exploring alternative battery chemistries, such as sodium-ion batteries, which rely on more abundant and less expensive materials. Additionally, solid-state batteries, which replace the flammable liquid electrolytes with solid materials, offer greater safety and higher energy density. Beyond batteries, there are numerous other promising energy storage solutions on the horizon. Flow batteries, for instance, store energy in electrolyte solutions that are pumped through specialized cells. They are particularly well-suited for largescale energy storage applications, like grid-level storage, as they can be scaled to meet the demands of different needs. Compressed air energy storage (CAES) is another innovative technology. This method involves compressing air when energy is abundant, storing it under high pressure, and releasing it to generate electricity when demand is high. CAES systems are particularly attractive for their long duration storage capabilities and ability to leverage existing infrastructure. Furthermore, advancements in hydrogen fuel cell technology hold significant potential for energy storage. Hydrogen fuel cells convert hydrogen gas into electricity through a chemical reaction, producing only water as a by-product. This makes them an incredibly clean energy source, with the potential to power vehicles, homes, and industries. The development of efficient and affordable hydrogen production methods is crucial for unlocking the full potential of this technology. Research is underway to improve the efficiency of electrolysis, a process that uses electricity to split water molecules into hydrogen and oxygen. While energy storage solutions are rapidly evolving, there are still significant challenges to overcome. One key hurdle is the cost of deploying these technologies on a large scale. Scaling up production, improving efficiency, and reducing costs are critical for achieving widespread adoption. Furthermore, there are regulatory and infrastructure challenges to address. Integrating these new technologies into existing energy grids requires careful planning and coordination. Moreover, there is a need to develop appropriate standards and regulations for ensuring the safety and reliability of energy storage systems. Despite the challenges, the future of energy storage is brimming with exciting possibilities. Technological advancements are continuously pushing the boundaries of what's achievable, leading to more efficient, cost-effective, and sustainable energy solutions. As we move towards a cleaner and more sustainable future, these innovations will play a pivotal role in ensuring that energy is readily available, affordable, and accessible for all. In the coming decades, we can expect to see a revolution in the way we store and manage energy. Batteries will become smaller, lighter, and more powerful, enabling everything from electric cars with longer ranges to portable devices that last for days. Hydrogen fuel cells will be integrated into our transportation systems, making clean and efficient energy accessible to all. The transition to a sustainable energy future will require a concerted effort from governments, industry, and individuals. By investing in research and development, fostering innovation, and adopting new technologies, we can unlock the full potential of energy storage and build a brighter and more sustainable future for generations to come.

The Future of Energy Consumption

The future of energy consumption is a complex and multifaceted topic that requires a careful examination of various factors, including global energy demand, technological advancements, and policy initiatives. As the world population continues to grow and economies expand, the demand for energy is expected to rise significantly in the coming decades. This presents a significant challenge for our planet, as it requires a transition toward more sustainable and efficient energy sources. One of the key drivers of energy consumption is economic growth. As countries develop and their populations become more affluent, their energy consumption tends to increase. This is particularly evident in emerging economies, where rapid industrialization and urbanization are leading to a surge in energy demand. For example, China, India, and other developing nations are experiencing substantial growth in their energy consumption, fueled by rising industrial production, transportation, and household energy use. However, the growth in energy demand is not limited to emerging economies. Even developed nations, such as the United States and European countries, continue to consume considerable amounts of energy. While these countries have made strides in improving energy efficiency, the increasing reliance on technology and digital services, along with the growth of transportation sectors, contributes to sustained energy consumption levels. Technology plays a crucial role in managing energy demand and promoting sustainable energy consumption. Advancements in energy efficiency technologies, such as LED lighting, smart appliances, and energy-efficient buildings, can help reduce overall energy consumption without compromising living standards. For instance, the widespread adoption of LED lighting has resulted in significant energy savings compared to traditional incandescent bulbs. Similarly, smart appliances, equipped with sensors and software that optimize their energy consumption, can reduce energy waste in households and commercial buildings. Moreover, technological innovation is driving the development of renewable energy sources, such as solar, wind, and hydro power. These sources have the potential to significantly reduce our reliance on fossil fuels, which are major contributors to greenhouse gas emissions and climate change. Solar photovoltaic technology, for example, has advanced rapidly, with the cost of solar panels decreasing significantly in recent years. This has made solar energy more affordable and accessible to a wider range of consumers. Wind energy has also witnessed substantial growth, with wind turbines becoming more efficient and capable of generating larger amounts of electricity. However, integrating renewable energy sources into existing power grids presents challenges. Renewable energy sources are often intermittent, meaning their output can vary depending on weather conditions. This requires advanced energy storage solutions, such as batteries and pumped hydro, to ensure a reliable and stable electricity supply. The development of efficient and cost-effective energy storage technologies is essential for the widespread adoption of renewable energy. Another crucial aspect of managing energy consumption is demand-side management. This involves implementing strategies to reduce energy consumption during peak demand periods, thereby minimizing the need for additional power generation. Smart grids, which use advanced sensors and communication technologies, can play a vital role in demand-side management. By providing consumers with real-time data on their energy consumption, smart grids empower them to make informed decisions about their energy usage. For example, consumers can adjust their energy usage patterns during peak demand periods, reducing strain on the power grid and minimizing the need for expensive power plants. Furthermore, policy initiatives are essential for promoting sustainable energy consumption. Governments can implement policies that encourage the adoption of energy efficiency technologies, provide incentives for renewable energy development, and regulate carbon emissions. Carbon pricing mechanisms, such as carbon taxes and cap-and-trade programs, can incentivize businesses and individuals to reduce their carbon footprints. Subsidies for renewable energy projects can encourage investment in clean energy technologies. The future of energy consumption will be shaped by a complex interplay of technological innovation, economic growth, and policy initiatives. As the global population continues to grow and energy demand rises, it is crucial to invest in sustainable energy solutions and implement policies that promote energy efficiency and reduce greenhouse gas emissions. The adoption of renewable energy sources, advancements in energy storage technologies, and the implementation of smart grids are all key components of a sustainable energy future. In conclusion, the future of energy consumption is inextricably linked to the advancements in technology, global economic trends, and policy decisions. Managing energy demand effectively, promoting sustainable energy sources, and incentivizing energy efficiency are essential for ensuring a sustainable and prosperous future. By embracing innovative technologies and implementing responsible policies, we can navigate the challenges and opportunities of the future of energy consumption and build a more sustainable and resilient energy system for generations to come.

Chapter Four

Biotechnology and Genetic Engineering

Introduction to Biotechnology

Biotechnology, a field that has emerged as a powerful force in reshaping our understanding and manipulation of life itself, is fundamentally about harnessing the power of living organisms and their biological processes for practical applications. It's a vast and diverse field encompassing a wide array of technologies that have revolutionized various sectors, including medicine, agriculture, and industry. At its core, biotechnology is about understanding the intricate workings of living systems, from the molecular level to the complex interactions within ecosystems. This knowledge empowers us to manipulate and engineer these systems to achieve specific goals. Imagine a world where diseases that once ravaged humanity are now eradicated, where food production is optimized to feed a growing global population, and where environmental pollution is effectively tackled using biological solutions. This is the promise of biotechnology, a field brimming with potential to address some of the most pressing challenges facing our planet. The Foundation of Biotechnology: A Journey from Simple to Complex The roots of biotechnology are deeply embedded in the history of human civilization. Our earliest ancestors instinctively utilized biological processes for survival. Think of the ancient practice of fermentation for making bread, wine, and cheese, or the selection of desired traits in crops through traditional breeding methods. These seemingly simple practices, while seemingly basic, are the seeds from which the vast field of biotechnology grew. But the true revolution in biotechnology began with the advent of molecular biology in the mid-20th century. The unravelling of the structure of DNA, the molecule that carries the genetic blueprint of life, marked a turning point. This breakthrough opened the door to a new era of understanding and manipulating the very essence of life. Key Areas of Impact: A Multifaceted Field Biotechnology's impact spans a multitude of sectors, each with its own unique set of innovations and applications. Let's delve into some of the key areas where biotechnology is making a difference: Medicine: The revolution in medical biotechnology has led to an unprecedented ability to diagnose, treat, and even prevent diseases. Genetic testing, for example, allows us to identify individuals at risk for certain genetic conditions, enabling early interventions and personalized treatment plans. Vaccines, once a miracle of modern medicine, are now developed using sophisticated biotechnological approaches, leading to the eradication of diseases like smallpox and a significant reduction in the incidence of polio. The development of monoclonal antibodies, powerful proteins that target specific disease-causing agents, has transformed the treatment of cancer and autoimmune disorders. Furthermore, gene therapy, a revolutionary approach that aims to correct genetic defects at their core, holds immense promise for treating a wide range of inherited diseases. The ability to modify the human genome through techniques like CRISPR-Cas9 is opening up a new frontier in medicine, offering the possibility of curing diseases that were once considered incurable. Agriculture: The impact of biotechnology on agriculture has been equally profound, leading to significant improvements in crop yields and disease resistance. Genetic engineering allows for the introduction of beneficial traits, such as herbicide resistance, pest resistance, and enhanced nutritional content, into crops. Bio fertilizers and bio pesticides, produced using microorganisms, offer eco-friendly alternatives to traditional chemical-based solutions, reducing environmental damage and promoting sustainable farming practices. The development of drought-tolerant and heat-resistant crops is crucial in mitigating the impacts of climate change on food security. With the increasing global population and the pressure on resources, biotechnology holds the key to ensuring food security for future generations. Industry: Biotechnology has found its way into various industries, from the production of biofuels to the development of bioremediation technologies for cleaning up pollution. The use of microorganisms to break down pollutants, such as oil spills or heavy metals, is a promising approach to environmental clean-up. Bioplastics, made from renewable resources like corn starch or sugar, offer a sustainable alternative to traditional plastics derived from fossil fuels, contributing to a greener future. The use of enzymes, biological catalysts, in various industrial processes is leading to more efficient and environmentally friendly manufacturing methods.

Unravelling the Secrets of Life:

The Science Behind Biotechnology The foundations of biotechnology lie in the intricate world of molecular biology, a field that explores the fundamental building blocks of life. At the heart of it all is DNA, the molecule that carries the genetic blueprint of every living organism. Understanding DNA structure and function is crucial for unlocking the secrets of life and harnessing its potential for human benefit.

DNA:

The Code of Life: DNA is a long, double-stranded molecule that resembles a twisted ladder. Each rung of the ladder consists of a pair of chemical bases: adenine (A) paired with thymine (T), and guanine (G) paired with cytosine (C). This specific sequence of bases forms the genetic code that determines the characteristics of every organism. It dictates the production of proteins, which are the workhorses of the cell, carrying out a wide range of functions. Gene Expression: The Key to Function: The process of gene expression, where information encoded in DNA is used to create proteins, is a complex symphony of molecular events. First, a copy of the DNA sequence, known as messenger RNA (mRNA), is created. This mRNA molecule then travels to the ribosome, the protein-making machinery of the cell, where it's used as a template for protein synthesis. This intricate process, tightly regulated by a complex network of molecules, ensures that the right proteins are produced at the right time and in the right amounts. Biotechnology Tools: The Arsenal of Modern Biology The field of biotechnology has been revolutionized by the development of powerful tools that enable us to manipulate and analyze biological systems with unprecedented precision. These tools have opened up new avenues for research, diagnosis, and treatment, pushing the boundaries of what we can achieve with biological systems. Here are some of the key tools used in biotechnology:

Genetic Engineering: Genetic engineering, a cornerstone of modern biotechnology, involves the direct manipulation of an organism's genetic material. This powerful technique allows for the introduction of new genes, the modification of existing genes, or the deletion of genes. Through these techniques, scientists can enhance desirable traits, such as crop yields, disease resistance, or therapeutic properties, or correct genetic defects that cause disease. Genetic engineering has become a fundamental tool in diverse fields, from agriculture and medicine to industrial biotechnology.

CRISPR-Cas9:

A Revolutionary Gene Editing Tool: The discovery of CRISPR-Cas9, a revolutionary gene editing technology, has transformed the field of biotechnology. This system, derived from bacteria's natural defence mechanism against viruses, allows scientists to target and modify specific DNA sequences with remarkable precision. CRISPR-Cas9 has the potential to revolutionize medicine by enabling the correction of genetic defects responsible for a wide range of diseases. It's also being explored for applications in agriculture, such as enhancing crop yields and disease resistance. The potential of CRISPR-Cas9 is immense, but it also raises ethical considerations about the potential for unintended consequences. **Bioinformatics and Genomics:** Bioinformatics, the integration of computer science and biology, plays a crucial role in modern biotechnology. It enables scientists to analyze vast amounts of biological data, including DNA sequences, protein structures, and gene expression patterns. Genomics, the study of entire genomes, has revolutionized our understanding of the genetic basis of disease and has enabled the development of personalized medicine approaches. Bioinformatics tools are essential for understanding complex biological processes and identifying potential drug targets.

Synthetic Biology:

Building New Biological Systems: Synthetic biology, a relatively new but rapidly growing field, focuses on the design and construction of new biological systems or modifying existing ones. Scientists use synthetic biology to create new biological parts, devices, and systems with specific functionalities. Applications range from engineering microorganisms for the production of biofuels and pharmaceuticals to developing novel biosensors for environmental monitoring. Synthetic biology holds immense promise for addressing global challenges, but it also raises ethical considerations about the potential for unintended consequences.

Ethical Considerations: Navigating the Uncharted Waters of Biotechnology The rapid advancements in biotechnology have sparked intense debates about the ethical implications of manipulating life itself. While the potential benefits are immense, it's crucial to approach these technologies with caution and a strong sense of responsibility. Ethical considerations in biotechnology cover a wide range of issues, including:

Genetic Modification of Humans: The potential to modify human genes raises profound ethical questions. While gene editing could cure diseases and enhance human capabilities, it also raises concerns about creating genetic inequalities and playing God with the human genome. The ethical implications of modifying the human germline, changes that could be passed down to future generations, require careful consideration and open public discourse.

Access to Biotechnology:

Equity and Fairness: The benefits of biotechnology should be accessible to all, regardless of their socioeconomic status or geographic location. Ensuring equitable access to genetic testing, gene therapy, and other biotechnological advancements is a critical ethical imperative. The potential for the development of a two-tiered healthcare system, where the wealthy have access to cutting-edge treatments while the poor are left behind, is a serious concern.

Environmental Impacts: Biotechnology has the potential to address environmental challenges, but it's crucial to assess its potential risks. The release of genetically modified organisms into the environment could have unintended consequences, disrupting ecosystems and potentially causing harm to biodiversity. Careful risk assessments and monitoring are essential to ensure that biotechnology is used sustainably and responsibly.

Intellectual Property and Access to Research: The complex web of patents and intellectual property rights associated with biotechnology can hinder research and limit access to life-saving treatments. Striking a balance between protecting intellectual property and ensuring access to vital technologies is essential for promoting innovation and ensuring that biotechnology benefits humanity as a whole.

The Future of Biotechnology: A World of Possibilities The future of biotechnology is bright, with a vast landscape of potential applications waiting to be explored. From curing diseases that have plagued humanity for centuries to addressing global challenges like climate change and food security, biotechnology holds immense promise for shaping a better future. Here are some areas where we can expect to see significant advancements in the coming years: **Personalized Medicine:** The rise of personalized medicine, tailored to the individual's unique genetic makeup, is one of the most exciting developments in biotechnology. By understanding an individual's genetic profile, doctors can develop treatments that are more effective and targeted, reducing side effects and improving patient outcomes. Personalized medicine has the potential to revolutionize healthcare, leading to more precise diagnoses, preventative interventions, and targeted therapies.

Synthetic Biology and Bio manufacturing: Synthetic biology is poised to transform the way we manufacture products, from pharmaceuticals to biofuels. Engineered microorganisms can be used as mini-factories to produce valuable chemicals, materials, and even fuels more sustainably than traditional industrial methods. Synthetic biology is opening up new possibilities for sustainable production, reducing our reliance on fossil fuels and mitigating environmental impact.

Biomaterials and Tissue Engineering: Biotechnology is enabling the development of novel biomaterials with unique properties and the creation of artificial tissues for transplantation. These innovations have the potential to revolutionize the treatment of injuries and diseases, offering new solutions for organ failure and tissue regeneration. Biomaterials are also being used to develop new drug delivery systems, enhancing the effectiveness of medications and reducing side effects.

Bioremediation and Environmental Sustainability: Biotechnology is playing an increasingly important role in addressing environmental challenges, from cleaning up pollution to restoring ecosystems. Bioremediation techniques, using microorganisms to break down pollutants, offer a sustainable and environmentally friendly approach to pollution control. Biotechnology can also help to restore degraded ecosystems, such as polluted waterways or depleted forests, by promoting the growth of beneficial microorganisms and plants. **Conclusion:** Embracing the Potential of Biotechnology, Biotechnology is a powerful force shaping our world, offering unprecedented opportunities to address some of the most pressing challenges facing humanity. From revolutionizing medicine to improving food security and cleaning up the environment, biotechnology has the potential to make a significant positive impact on our lives. However, it's crucial to approach these technologies with a sense of responsibility, considering their ethical implications and ensuring equitable access to their benefits. By fostering open dialogue, promoting responsible research, and harnessing the power of biotechnology for the betterment of humankind, we can create a brighter future for generations to come.

Gene Editing and CRISPR Technology

Imagine a world where we can rewrite the very blueprint of life, correcting genetic flaws that cause devastating diseases, enhancing human capabilities, and even designing organisms with novel functionalities. This is the promise of gene editing, a revolutionary technology that has taken the scientific world by storm. At the heart of this revolution lies CRISPR-Cas9, a powerful tool that allows us to precisely target and alter specific genes with unprecedented accuracy and efficiency. CRISPR-Cas9, a name that sounds more like a sci-fi invention than a real-world technology, is derived from the natural defence system of bacteria. These microscopic organisms use CRISPR to combat viral infections, storing snippets of viral DNA in their own genomes as a "memory" of past invaders. When a virus attacks again, the bacterial cells use the stored genetic information to create guide RNA molecules that, in partnership with Cas9, a protein enzyme, specifically target and destroy the invading viral DNA. In essence, CRISPR-Cas9 is a molecular scissor that allows us to cut and paste DNA sequences with astonishing precision. Scientists have harnessed this natural system for a range of ground breaking applications, including: Genetic Disease Treatment: By correcting faulty genes, CRISPR-Cas9 holds the potential to cure genetic diseases like cystic fibrosis, Huntington's disease, sickle cell anaemia, and muscular dystrophy. Imagine a future where these debilitating conditions are no longer a life sentence. Cancer Therapy: CRISPR-Cas9 is being explored as a weapon against cancer by precisely targeting and disabling genes that drive tumour growth. This approach promises to revolutionize cancer treatment, offering more effective and less toxic therapies. Agricultural Advancements: CRISPR-Cas9 has the power to improve crop yields, enhance nutritional content, and even engineer crops that are resistant to pests and diseases. This could significantly impact global food security, particularly in regions facing food shortages. Biofuel Production: Engineering algae and other organisms to produce biofuels using CRISPR-Cas9 could offer a more sustainable and environmentally friendly alternative to fossil fuels. Biomaterial Engineering: CRISPR-Cas9 can be used to create designer proteins and tissues for medical implants, regenerative medicine, and drug delivery systems. Disease Prevention: By altering the genetic makeup of disease vectors like mosquitoes, CRISPR-Cas9 could potentially eliminate diseases like malaria and dengue fever, saving millions of lives.

The impact of CRISPR-Cas9 technology is not just confined to the laboratory; it's already shaping our world in tangible ways. Genetically Engineered Crops: CRISPR-Cas9 is being used to create crops with desirable traits, such as resistance to herbicides and improved nutritional content. These crops are already on the market, offering farmers greater efficiency and sustainability. Improved Livestock: CRISPR-Cas9 is being used to enhance livestock traits, such as disease resistance and increased milk production, improving livestock productivity and reducing the need for antibiotics. Diagnostic Tools: CRISPR-Cas9 is being used to develop sensitive and rapid diagnostic tools for various diseases, enabling faster and more accurate disease detection. The implications of CRISPR-Cas9 are far-reaching and profound, touching upon some of the most fundamental questions about life, health, and society. This technology raises ethical considerations that demand careful attention and responsible research practices: Genetic Modification of Humans: The possibility of editing human embryos to correct genetic defects raises ethical concerns about designer babies and the potential for unintended consequences. Access and Equity: Ensuring that the benefits of CRISPRCas9 are available to all, regardless of their economic background, is crucial to prevent a widening gap in healthcare access. Environmental Risks: The unintended consequences of genetically engineered organisms on the environment need careful consideration to prevent ecological disruptions. Regulation and Oversight: Clear and robust regulatory frameworks are essential to ensure responsible use of CRISPR-Cas9 technology and prevent its misuse. CRISPR-Cas9 is not without limitations, and its application requires careful consideration of its potential benefits and risks. Off-target Editing: One concern is the possibility of unintended edits in non-target regions of the genome, which could lead to unforeseen consequences. Delivery Challenges: Efficient and targeted delivery of the CRISPR-Cas9 system to specific cells and tissues remains a challenge, especially in vivo. Ethical Considerations: The ethical implications of gene editing, particularly in humans, are complex and require ongoing discussions among scientists, ethicists, and policymakers. Despite these challenges, the potential of CRISPR-Cas9 to revolutionize various fields is undeniable. Its ability to manipulate the very building blocks of life opens up unprecedented possibilities for improving human health, addressing environmental challenges, and shaping our future. As we continue to explore the capabilities of this revolutionary technology, we must proceed with caution, ensuring responsible research, ethical considerations, and thoughtful public discourse. The future of CRISPR-Cas9 lies in our hands, and the choices we make today will determine its impact on generations to come.

Synthetic Biology and Its Implications

Synthetic biology, a relatively new field within biotechnology, is pushing the boundaries of what we can achieve by manipulating and engineering biological systems. It envisions a future where we can design and build new organisms with tailored functionalities, much like we program computers. This field holds tremendous promise for addressing some of humanity's most pressing challenges, from developing sustainable energy sources to producing novel pharmaceuticals and materials. At its core, synthetic biology seeks to understand and control the building blocks of life, DNA and proteins, to create entirely new biological systems or modify existing ones. Imagine creating a new microbe designed to produce biofuels from agricultural waste, or engineering bacteria to clean up toxic pollutants from contaminated soil. These are just a few examples of the many potential applications of synthetic biology. One of the key tools in synthetic biology is the ability to manipulate genetic code. CRISPR-Cas9 technology, a revolutionary gene-editing tool, has made it easier than ever to precisely edit DNA sequences, enabling scientists to introduce specific modifications in organisms. This technology has opened doors to a wide range of applications, from developing new disease therapies to engineering crops resistant to pests and diseases. However, the potential of synthetic biology extends far beyond gene editing. Researchers are also working on developing synthetic biological systems from scratch, constructing those using artificial DNA sequences. This involves designing and assembling DNA fragments like building blocks, then introducing them into cells to create new biological circuits and functions. These synthetic biological systems could potentially perform complex tasks, such as sensing environmental changes and triggering specific responses, providing a range of possibilities for applications in medicine, agriculture, and environmental protection. Here are some examples of how synthetic biology is already making a difference: Biofuel production: Synthetic biology is being used to engineer microbes that can efficiently convert plant biomass, agricultural waste, or even carbon dioxide into biofuels. This has the potential to reduce our reliance on fossil fuels and mitigate climate change. Environmental remediation: Scientists are developing synthetic microbes capable of degrading pollutants like pesticides, heavy metals, or plastic waste. These organisms could play a crucial role in cleaning up contaminated environments. Drug development: Synthetic biology is being utilized to create new therapeutic agents, including antibodies, enzymes, and vaccines. This involves engineering microbes to produce specific proteins with desired therapeutic properties. Food security: Synthetic biology can be used to improve crop yields by developing plants that are resistant to pests, diseases, or harsh environmental conditions. This can contribute to increased food production and improved food security. However, with great potential comes great responsibility. The ethical and societal implications of synthetic biology require careful consideration. One of the most pressing concerns is the potential for misuse, such as creating biological weapons or releasing genetically modified organisms into the environment with unpredictable consequences. Moreover, the potential for unintended consequences is a significant concern. Even with careful design, engineered organisms could evolve in unexpected ways, leading to unforeseen impacts on ecosystems or human health. Another ethical dilemma arises from the potential to create synthetic life forms that could blur the lines between natural and artificial, raising questions about the nature of life itself. To address these challenges, it is crucial to foster open dialogue and collaboration among scientists, policymakers, and the public. This will help establish ethical guidelines and regulatory frameworks that ensure the responsible development and application of synthetic biology. Here are some key ethical considerations: Biosafety and biosecurity: Ensuring that engineered organisms are safe and secure, preventing accidental releases or intentional misuse. Environmental impact: Assessing the potential ecological consequences of introducing synthetic organisms into the environment. Public engagement: Involving the public in discussions about the potential benefits and risks of synthetic biology. Intellectual property rights: Addressing the ethical and legal considerations surrounding the ownership and commercialization of synthetic biological systems. As synthetic biology continues to advance, it is essential to strike a balance between innovation and responsible stewardship. By carefully navigating the ethical and societal challenges, we can harness the transformative power of this technology to address some of the world's most pressing challenges and shape a brighter future for humanity. One area where synthetic biology is making significant strides is in the development of personalized medicine. By combining synthetic biology techniques with genetic testing, doctors can now tailor treatments to individual patients based on their unique genetic makeup. This personalized approach to healthcare holds the promise of more effective and less toxic therapies. For example, synthetic biologists are developing cell-based therapies, using engineered cells to deliver targeted therapies to specific tissues or organs. This approach has shown promise in treating various conditions, including cancer, genetic disorders, and autoimmune diseases. Another emerging area of research in synthetic biology is the development of biomaterials. By engineering biological systems to produce novel materials, scientists aim to create sustainable alternatives to traditional materials derived from fossil fuels. These biomaterials could find applications in a wide range of industries, from textiles and construction to medical implants and electronics. The future of synthetic biology is full of possibilities. As our understanding of biology continues to grow and technological advancements accelerate, we can expect even more ground breaking discoveries and applications. However, it is crucial to remain vigilant and ensure that the development of synthetic biology is guided by ethical considerations and responsible stewardship. Only then can we harness the transformative power of this technology for the benefit of humanity and our planet. In conclusion, synthetic biology is a rapidly evolving field with immense potential to address some of humanity's most pressing challenges. By manipulating and engineering biological systems, we can create new solutions for healthcare, energy, food security, and environmental protection. However, it is crucial to recognize the ethical and societal implications of this powerful technology and ensure its responsible development and application. By fostering open dialogue and collaboration among stakeholders, we can navigate the ethical challenges and harness the transformative power of synthetic biology to create a brighter future for all.

Personalized Medicine and Healthcare

The burgeoning field of biotechnology is rapidly transforming healthcare, ushering in an era of personalized medicine. This revolutionary approach promises to tailor medical treatments to the individual, taking into account their unique genetic makeup, lifestyle, and environmental factors. At its core lies the idea that one-size-fits-all treatments are no longer the most effective way to address the diverse needs of patients. Imagine a world where your doctor analyzes your genetic code to identify specific vulnerabilities and prescribe the most effective drug therapies. This is the vision that personalized medicine strives to achieve, leveraging the power of biotechnology to unlock a new era of precision healthcare. The foundation of personalized medicine lies in the understanding of our genes and their intricate roles in health and disease. Through techniques like gene sequencing, scientists can now map the entire human genome, uncovering variations that may predispose individuals to certain ailments or influence their response to specific medications. This information empowers doctors to make more informed diagnoses, predict disease risk, and recommend individualized treatment plans. One prominent example of this paradigm shift is the development of pharmacogenomics, a branch of personalized medicine that focuses on tailoring drug therapies based on an individual's genetic makeup. By analyzing specific genes that influence drug metabolism and response, pharmacogenomics helps predict how a patient will metabolize a drug and whether it will be effective for their specific condition. This approach not only improves treatment outcomes but also minimizes side effects, reducing the risk of adverse reactions. Beyond diagnostics and drug therapy, personalized medicine extends its reach to other areas of healthcare, including preventive care and disease management. By identifying individuals at high risk for specific diseases based on their genetic predispositions, doctors can implement early intervention strategies to delay or even prevent the onset of these ailments. This proactive approach has the potential to significantly improve public health outcomes and reduce healthcare costs in the long run. The use of genomic information in personalized medicine is not without its challenges. Ethical considerations surrounding data privacy and potential discrimination based on genetic information are paramount. Ensuring the equitable access to personalized medicine for all individuals, regardless of their socioeconomic background, is also crucial to prevent further healthcare disparities. Despite these challenges, personalized medicine holds immense promise for the future of healthcare. Its ability to predict disease, personalize treatment plans, and optimize patient outcomes represents a transformative shift in how we approach medical care. As biotechnology continues to advance, we can expect to see even more innovative applications of personalized medicine, further revolutionizing the healthcare landscape. The Role of Biotechnology in Personalized Medicine The development of personalized medicine is inextricably linked to the advancements in biotechnology. Several key areas of biotechnology contribute significantly to this revolution:

1. Gene Sequencing: Gene sequencing technology has been instrumental in revolutionizing personalized medicine by allowing us to map the entire human genome and identify specific genetic variations. This information provides a wealth of data for understanding individual differences in health and disease susceptibility.

2. Gene Editing: Gene editing technologies like CRISPRCas9 have opened new avenues for treating genetic diseases. By precisely targeting and modifying specific genes, CRISPR-Cas9 holds the potential to cure genetic disorders that were once considered incurable. This technology is also being explored for developing novel gene therapies for a wide range of diseases, including cancer and infectious diseases.

3. Biomarkers: Biomarkers are specific biological molecules or characteristics that can be used to identify the presence, severity, or progression of a disease. These biomarkers can be used to personalize diagnosis and treatment plans, as well as to monitor disease progression and response to therapy. Biotechnology plays a vital role in developing and utilizing these biomarkers for personalized healthcare.

4. Proteomics: Proteomics is the study of the complete set of proteins produced by an organism, known as the proteome. By analyzing the proteome, researchers can gain insights into the complex processes that govern health and disease. This information can be utilized to develop personalized therapies that target specific proteins involved in disease pathogenesis.

5. Microbiome Analysis: The human microbiome, the vast collection of microbes that reside in our bodies, plays a significant role in maintaining health. Biotechnology is enabling scientists to study and understand the microbiome, leading to the development of personalized therapies that target these microbial communities. This includes the use of probiotics and prebiotics to modulate the microbiome and promote gut health, ultimately influencing overall wellbeing. Examples of Personalized Medicine in Action: The impact of personalized medicine is already being felt in various areas of healthcare, with numerous examples highlighting its transformative potential:

1. Cancer Treatment: Personalized medicine is revolutionizing cancer treatment by enabling oncologists to tailor therapies based on the specific genetic mutations driving the tumour's growth. Genomic profiling of cancer cells helps identify the key molecular targets for targeted therapies, maximizing treatment efficacy and minimizing side effects.

2. Drug Development: The development of personalized medicine has fostered a shift towards targeted drug therapies that specifically address the underlying molecular causes of disease. This approach has led to the development of innovative drugs that are highly effective in treating specific diseases, often with fewer side effects compared to traditional treatments.

3. Rare Diseases: Personalized medicine offers hope for patients with rare diseases, often characterized by unique genetic mutations. By understanding the underlying genetic causes of these diseases, researchers can develop targeted therapies that address the specific needs of these patient populations.

4. Cardiovascular Disease: Personalized medicine is playing a crucial role in managing cardiovascular disease, one of the leading causes of death worldwide. Genetic testing can help identify individuals at high risk for heart disease, enabling doctors to implement preventive measures and personalized treatment plans to reduce their risk of developing cardiovascular events.

5. Mental Health: The application of personalized medicine in mental health is an emerging area, with promising potential for improving diagnosis and treatment of mental disorders. Genetic testing can help identify individuals who may be at risk for specific mental disorders, and it can also be used to personalize treatment plans based on individual genetic profiles. Ethical Considerations in Personalized Medicine While the potential benefits of personalized medicine are undeniable, it's crucial to acknowledge and address the ethical considerations that arise from its implementation. These include: 1. Privacy and Data Security: Personalized medicine relies heavily on genetic information, which raises concerns about privacy and data security. It's essential to establish robust safeguards to protect this sensitive data from unauthorized access and misuse. 2. Equity and Accessibility: Ensuring that personalized medicine is accessible to everyone, regardless of socioeconomic background, is crucial to prevent further healthcare disparities. The high cost of genetic testing and personalized therapies can create a barrier to access, potentially exacerbating existing health inequalities. 3. Potential for Discrimination: The use of genetic information in personalized medicine raises concerns about potential discrimination based on genetic predispositions. It's important to establish clear guidelines and regulations to prevent misuse of this information for purposes such as employment, insurance, or social exclusion. 4. Informed Consent: Patients must be fully informed about the potential benefits and risks of personalized medicine, including the potential for unforeseen consequences or ethical dilemmas. Informed consent is crucial to ensure that patients make informed decisions about their healthcare. The Future of Personalized Medicine Personalized medicine is a rapidly evolving field with immense potential for transforming healthcare. Future advancements in biotechnology will likely lead to even more sophisticated personalized approaches, with implications for various aspects of healthcare, including:

1. Predictive Medicine: The ability to predict disease risk based on genetic information and lifestyle factors will become increasingly refined, enabling proactive measures to prevent or delay the onset of diseases.

2. Targeted Therapies: The development of targeted therapies that specifically address the underlying molecular causes of disease will continue to advance, leading to more effective treatments with fewer side effects.

3. Artificial Intelligence and Machine Learning: AI and machine learning will play a growing role in analyzing vast amounts of genetic and clinical data, identifying patterns and predicting disease outcomes. This will enable more precise diagnosis, treatment planning, and disease management.

4. Biotechnology and Regenerative Medicine: The convergence of biotechnology and regenerative medicine holds immense promise for developing novel therapies that repair damaged tissues and organs. This could revolutionize treatment for conditions that were once considered incurable. The future of personalized medicine is brimming with possibilities, paving the way for a healthcare system that is truly patient-centered and tailored to individual needs. However, it's essential to address the ethical challenges and ensure equitable access to these ground breaking technologies. By navigating these complexities, we can harness the power of personalized medicine to improve health outcomes for all.

Ethical and Societal Challenges

The ethical considerations surrounding biotechnology and genetic engineering are complex and multifaceted, reflecting the profound impact these technologies have on our understanding of life itself. As we delve deeper into the intricacies of manipulating the building blocks of life, we are confronted with ethical dilemmas that challenge our values and our perception of human nature. One of the most prominent ethical concerns revolves around the potential for genetic inequality. The ability to alter genes raises concerns about creating a society where access to advanced genetic technologies is limited to the wealthy or privileged, potentially leading to a widening gap between those with access to enhanced genes and those without. Imagine a world where only the affluent can afford to ensure their children are born with genes that confer heightened intelligence, resistance to diseases, or enhanced athletic abilities. Such a scenario could exacerbate existing social inequalities and create a genetic underclass, raising profound ethical questions about fairness, justice, and the very definition of human potential. The potential for unintended consequences is another major ethical concern. While CRISPR and other gene-editing tools offer the promise of treating and even preventing genetic diseases, there is a risk of introducing unforeseen genetic alterations that could have negative downstream effects. The complex web of interactions within our genetic code means that altering one gene can have unpredictable consequences for other genes and biological processes. This unpredictability necessitates cautious and rigorous research before implementing gene-editing therapies, particularly in the realm of germline editing, where changes to the genome can be passed down to future generations. The ethical implications of synthetic biology, which aims to engineer novel biological systems, also raise concerns. The creation of artificial life forms, while potentially beneficial for applications like bioremediation and bio manufacturing, raises profound questions about the boundaries of life and the potential for unintended consequences. What are the ethical implications of creating organisms that are not subject to the natural laws of evolution, or that could potentially escape from controlled environments and pose risks to existing ecosystems? These questions demand careful consideration and a robust ethical framework for guiding research and development in this field. The ethical landscape is further complicated by the issue of genetic enhancement. While gene editing holds promise for treating diseases, some argue that it could also be used to enhance human traits beyond the realm of health, potentially leading to a slippery slope toward designer babies and a narrow definition of human perfection. This raises complex questions about what constitutes a "desirable" trait and whether it is ethical to use genetic technologies to shape the characteristics of future generations. These concerns are particularly relevant in the context of reproductive technologies, where parents may have the ability to select certain genetic traits for their offspring. Beyond the ethical considerations surrounding individual choices, biotechnology and genetic engineering also raise questions about the collective responsibility of humanity. What is our collective duty to future generations in terms of ensuring the responsible use of these powerful technologies? How can we establish global agreements and regulations that balance the potential benefits of these technologies with the need to safeguard our shared genetic heritage? These are just a few of the ethical dilemmas that arise from the intersection of biotechnology and genetics. As these technologies continue to evolve at an unprecedented pace, it becomes increasingly important to engage in open and thoughtful discussions about their ethical implications. We must strive to develop a shared understanding of our values, and to establish ethical guidelines that ensure the responsible and equitable use of these transformative technologies. This requires a multidisciplinary approach, involving scientists, ethicists, policymakers, and members of the public, to address the complex social, ethical, and legal challenges posed by the burgeoning field of biotechnology and genetic engineering. The impact of biotechnology and genetic engineering extends far beyond the realm of individual choices and ethical dilemmas. It has the potential to fundamentally reshape our relationship with the natural world, altering the course of human evolution and the very definition of what it means to be human. As we explore the frontiers of genetic manipulation, we must engage in a broader societal dialogue about the implications of these technologies, not only for our own lives but for the future of humanity and the planet. The prospect of "playing God" has long been a source of anxiety and debate, and it takes on new meaning in the context of biotechnology and genetic engineering. While some see these technologies as offering unparalleled opportunities to improve human health and well-being, others view them with apprehension, fearing that they could be used to create a "perfect" human race or to widen the gap between the rich and the poor. The potential for unintended consequences and the erosion of human diversity are also points of concern. As we navigate this uncharted territory, it is essential to approach these technologies with a sense of humility and responsibility. The power to alter the very fabric of life is a profound responsibility, and it demands a careful balancing of scientific progress with ethical considerations. We must ensure that our pursuit of scientific advancement is guided by a deep respect for human dignity, diversity, and the interconnectedness of life on Earth. This requires engaging in open and transparent dialogues about the implications of these technologies, involving not only scientists and ethicists but also policymakers, religious leaders, and the general public. We must foster a culture of critical thinking and informed decision-making, ensuring that these powerful tools are used for the benefit of all humanity, rather than for the exclusive advantage of a select few. The ethical and societal challenges posed by biotechnology and genetic engineering are complex and evolving. As we delve deeper into the mysteries of life and the possibilities of manipulating its building blocks, it is crucial that we engage in a thoughtful and ongoing dialogue about the potential benefits and risks of these technologies. The future of humanity is inextricably linked to the choices we make today regarding these powerful tools. Our responsibility is to ensure that they are used for the betterment of all, while safeguarding the fundamental principles of human dignity, diversity, and the interconnectedness of life on Earth.

Chapter Five
The Digital Frontier

Augmented and Virtual Reality

Imagine stepping into a world where the lines between the physical and digital blur, where interactive experiences transport you to fantastical realms and enhance your everyday reality. This is the promise of augmented reality (AR) and virtual reality (VR), two transformative technologies poised to revolutionize how we interact with the world around us. AR overlays digital information onto our real-world view, seamlessly integrating virtual elements with our physical surroundings. Picture a scenario where you're walking down a street, and your phone screen displays directions overlaid on top of your real-time view. This is just one simple example of AR's potential. Imagine using your phone to scan a museum artefact and access its rich history, or using AR glasses to visualize complex anatomical structures for medical training. VR, on the other hand, immerses us in entirely virtual environments, transporting us to places that are geographically distant or even purely imaginary. With VR headsets, we can experience the thrill of skydiving, explore ancient ruins, or attend a virtual concert, all from the comfort of our own homes. VR has the potential to redefine entertainment, education, and training, creating experiences that are more engaging and immersive than ever before. The applications of AR and VR are vast and constantly evolving. Here's a glimpse into the transformative potential of these technologies across various sectors: Entertainment and Gaming: AR and VR are already making waves in the entertainment and gaming industries. Imagine immersive gaming experiences where you're no longer just watching on a screen but physically interacting with the game world. Imagine concerts where you can feel the energy of the crowd and experience the music as if you were right there in the venue. AR and VR have the power to elevate entertainment to new heights, blurring the lines between fantasy and reality. Education and Training: AR and VR offer unparalleled opportunities for education and training. Imagine students taking virtual field trips to explore historical sites or dissecting virtual organs to learn about human anatomy without the need for physical specimens. Imagine VR simulations for training surgeons or pilots, where they can practice complex procedures in a safe and controlled environment. AR and VR can revolutionize how we learn and acquire skills, making education more engaging and effective. Healthcare and Medical Applications: The applications of AR and VR in healthcare are truly ground breaking. Surgeons can use AR glasses to visualize real-time patient data during surgery, improving precision and efficiency. Patients recovering from injuries can engage in VR therapy to regain motor skills and manage pain. VR simulations can be used to train medical professionals in emergency procedures, providing a safe and realistic environment for learning and practicing. Retail and E-commerce: AR and VR are poised to revolutionize the retail and ecommerce experience. Imagine using your phone to virtually try on clothes before you buy them, or using VR to explore a virtual store and browse products from the comfort of your home. AR and VR can create immersive shopping experiences, allowing consumers to better visualize products and make informed purchasing decisions. Architecture and Design: AR and VR can transform the way architects and designers plan and present their projects. Imagine using AR glasses to visualize a proposed building design overlaid on the actual site, or using VR to create virtual walkthroughs of buildings before they are even constructed. This can facilitate collaboration, communication, and better decision-making in the design process. Manufacturing and Industry: AR and VR are already being adopted in manufacturing and industrial settings. Imagine workers using AR glasses to access real-time information about machinery or to receive step-by-step instructions for complex tasks. VR simulations can be used for training workers on new equipment or processes, reducing downtime and improving safety. Social Interaction and Communication: AR and VR are also poised to revolutionize how we interact with each other. Imagine using VR to hold virtual meetings or social gatherings, creating immersive and engaging experiences that transcend geographical boundaries. AR overlays can enhance communication by providing real-time translations or by adding context-specific information to our interactions. The development of AR and VR technologies is constantly progressing, pushing the boundaries of what's possible. We're already seeing advancements in hardware, software, and content development, leading to more immersive and interactive experiences. As these technologies continue to evolve, we can expect to see even more transformative applications emerge across diverse industries. Challenges and Ethical Considerations: While AR and VR offer tremendous potential, they also present challenges and ethical considerations that need to be addressed. Some of the key concerns include: Privacy and Data Security: AR and VR technologies collect vast amounts of personal data, raising concerns about privacy violations and the potential misuse of this information. Accessibility and Inclusivity: Ensuring that AR and VR technologies are accessible to all individuals, regardless of their physical abilities or socioeconomic status, is a crucial challenge. Addiction and Dependence: Excessive use of AR and VR technologies can lead to addiction and dependence, impacting individuals' physical and mental well-being. Social Isolation: Immersive virtual experiences could potentially lead to social isolation and a disconnect from real-world interactions. Ethical Implications of VR Simulations: VR simulations that involve violence or harmful activities raise ethical concerns about the potential for desensitization and the normalization of harmful behaviours. The Future of AR and VR: The future of AR and VR holds boundless possibilities. As these technologies mature, we can expect to see even more immersive, interactive, and impactful applications across various industries. We can anticipate the development of more advanced hardware, such as lighter and more comfortable headsets, as well as more realistic and engaging content. The future of AR and VR is likely to involve a convergence of these technologies with other cutting-edge advancements, such as AI, machine learning, and the Internet of Things. This convergence will create even more powerful and transformative applications, blurring the lines between the physical and digital realms. To harness the full potential of AR and VR, it's crucial to address the challenges and ethical considerations that come with these technologies. Responsible development and implementation are essential to ensure that these innovations benefit humanity and contribute to a better future. By carefully navigating the challenges and harnessing the transformative power of AR and VR, we can pave the way for a more immersive, engaging, and enriching world for generations to come.

G and the Internet of Things

This chapter takes us into a world where interconnected devices and lightning-fast networks redefine our interactions with technology and each other. We've already encountered how AI is transforming various aspects of our lives, but its full potential hinges on the ability to collect, process, and transmit vast amounts of data at incredible speeds. Enter 5G, the latest generation of wireless technology, and the Internet of Things (IoT), a vast network of interconnected devices, which together are poised to usher in a new era of connectedness. Imagine a world where your refrigerator automatically orders groceries when supplies run low, your car communicates with traffic lights to optimize your commute, and your home's lighting adjusts to your mood and activity levels. This is the promise of the IoT, where physical objects, from everyday appliances to industrial machinery, are embedded with sensors, software, and network connectivity, allowing them to interact with each other and their environment. The sheer scale and complexity of this interconnected ecosystem require a network that can handle the massive data flows and ensure seamless communication. This is where 5G comes in. 5G is not just an incremental upgrade from its predecessors. It represents a quantum leap in wireless technology, offering significantly faster speeds, lower latency, and increased capacity. It's like replacing a narrow, congested highway with a multi-lane superhighway designed for high-speed traffic. This dramatic improvement in connectivity is crucial for enabling the widespread adoption of IoT devices and unlocking their full potential. Think of 5G as the digital backbone supporting the IoT. It's the invisible network that enables devices to talk to each other, collect data, and act on it in real-time. This real-time communication is crucial for applications that demand immediate responses, such as autonomous vehicles, remote surgery, and industrial automation. Imagine a self-driving car relying on 5G to receive data from sensors and communicate with other vehicles on the road, navigating complex traffic situations with millisecond precision. This level of responsiveness wouldn't be possible without the speed and low latency of 5G. But the benefits of 5G and IoT extend far beyond individual devices and applications. Their impact is felt across entire industries, transforming how we live, work, and interact with the world around us. In healthcare, 5G and IoT enable the development of remote patient monitoring systems, allowing doctors to remotely track vital signs, provide virtual consultations, and respond to health emergencies in real time. This technology has the potential to revolutionize healthcare delivery, particularly in rural areas and underserved communities, by extending access to specialized medical care. Smart cities are another domain where 5G and IoT are making a transformative impact. By connecting streetlights, traffic sensors, and waste management systems, cities can optimize resource allocation, reduce energy consumption, and improve public safety. Imagine a city where streetlights automatically adjust brightness based on real-time traffic conditions, waste collection is optimized based on sensor data, and public safety is enhanced by real-time monitoring of crime hotspots. This interconnected web of data and sensors can create a more efficient, sustainable, and liveable urban environment. The industrial sector is also experiencing a dramatic shift with the advent of 5G and IoT. By connecting machines, sensors, and software, industries can automate processes, improve efficiency, and unlock new levels of productivity. Consider the example of a manufacturing plant where sensors on machines monitor performance and automatically adjust production parameters based on real-time data. This not only improves quality control but also optimizes resource utilization and reduces downtime. The integration of 5G and IoT in manufacturing is leading to the rise of smart factories, where data-driven insights and automation are transforming production processes. However, this brave new world of interconnected devices and lightning-fast networks comes with its own set of challenges. One of the most pressing concerns is cybersecurity. With more devices connected to the internet, the attack surface for hackers expands, creating vulnerabilities that can be exploited to steal data, disrupt operations, and even cause physical harm. Imagine a scenario where a hacker takes control of a city's traffic management system, causing chaos and gridlock. This underscores the critical need for robust cybersecurity measures to protect these interconnected systems from malicious actors. Privacy is another critical issue raised by the proliferation of connected devices. As IoT devices gather and transmit vast amounts of data about our lives, the potential for misuse and privacy violations grows. Imagine a scenario where your home's smart devices are used to track your movements, monitor your conversations, and even sell your personal data without your consent. This raises ethical questions about how we manage the vast amounts of data generated by IoT devices and ensure that it is used responsibly. Despite these challenges, the potential benefits of 5G and IoT are undeniable. They have the power to revolutionize industries, transform our cities, and improve our lives in countless ways. But to realize this full potential, we must address the ethical and security concerns that come with this new technological frontier. As we move further into the digital age, the interplay between 5G and IoT will continue to shape our world. It will be crucial to navigate these new technologies responsibly, balancing innovation with security, privacy, and ethical considerations. The future of connectivity hinges on our ability to harness the power of 5G and IoT to create a more efficient, sustainable, and equitable world for all.

Cybersecurity in the Digital Age

In the interconnected tapestry of the digital age, where information flows like a raging river and data is the new currency, a silent battle is waged – a war against the unseen forces that threaten to exploit our digital vulnerabilities. This is the realm of cybersecurity, a critical frontier where the defence of our online lives hinges on a delicate balance between technological prowess and human vigilance. Imagine a world where every device, from our smartphones to our refrigerators, is interconnected, forming an intricate web of communication and data exchange. This interconnectedness, while ushering in a new era of convenience and efficiency, also presents a fertile ground for cybercriminals. The Internet of Things (IoT), with its vast network of interconnected devices, has become a prime target for hackers seeking to exploit vulnerabilities and steal sensitive information. From smart home devices to medical implants, the potential consequences of a cyberattack can be devastating, ranging from data breaches to disruptions in critical infrastructure. Cybersecurity, therefore, is no longer a niche concern for tech-savvy individuals; it has become an integral part of our collective well-being. It is the shield that protects our digital assets, from our financial accounts to our personal data, from the relentless onslaught of cyber threats. The digital frontier is a battleground where the lines between the physical and virtual worlds are blurring, and cybersecurity is the indispensable weapon in this ever-evolving war. But what are the strategies that we can employ to fortify our defences in this digital battlefield? The answer lies in a multifaceted approach that combines technological innovations with human vigilance. Technological Safeguards: A Fortress of Innovation The first line of defence in the digital age is a robust arsenal of technological safeguards. These are the shields and moats that protect our digital castles, deterring attackers and minimizing the impact of successful intrusions. - Firewalls: The

First Line of Defence: Firewalls act as digital gatekeepers, scrutinizing incoming and outgoing network traffic, blocking unauthorized access and preventing malicious software from infiltrating our systems. These digital sentinels stand guard at the perimeter of our networks, filtering out harmful traffic before it can reach our valuable data.

- Anti-virus Software: The Antidote to Malware: Malware, a broad term encompassing viruses, worms, Trojans, and ransomware, is a persistent threat to our digital security. Anti-virus software acts as an antidote to these malicious entities, detecting and removing them from our systems, protecting us from their destructive capabilities.

- Intrusion Detection Systems (IDS): The Watchful Eye: IDSs work tirelessly to monitor our networks for suspicious activity, acting like vigilant guards who alert us to any unauthorized access or attempted breaches. These systems use advanced algorithms and anomaly detection techniques to identify potential threats, empowering us to react swiftly and minimize the damage.

- Encryption: Securing Our Digital Secrets: Encryption, the art of scrambling data into an unreadable format, is a cornerstone of cybersecurity. It adds an extra layer of protection, ensuring that even if malicious actors gain access to our data, they cannot decipher its contents without the appropriate decryption key.

- Multi-factor Authentication (MFA): An Extra Layer of Security: MFA adds an extra layer of security to our online accounts, requiring more than just a password to grant access. It typically involves a combination of factors, such as a password, a unique code sent to our phone, or a fingerprint scan. This multi-faceted approach makes it significantly harder for unauthorized individuals to gain access to our accounts. Human Vigilance: The Unwavering Guardian While technological safeguards form the foundation of our digital security, human vigilance remains an indispensable component in the battle against cyber threats. Cybercriminals are adept at exploiting human vulnerabilities, using social engineering techniques to trick unsuspecting individuals into revealing sensitive information or granting access to their systems. Therefore, a well-informed and vigilant population is the most effective countermeasure against these insidious attacks.

- Password Hygiene: The Foundation of Digital Security: A strong password is the first line of defence against unauthorized access to our accounts. Avoid using easily guessed passwords like "password" or "123456". Instead, opt for long and complex passwords that incorporate a mix of uppercase and lowercase letters, numbers, and symbols. Consider using a password manager to store and manage your passwords securely, freeing you from the burden of remembering numerous intricate combinations.

- Phishing Awareness: Recognizing the Red Flags: Phishing attacks, disguised as legitimate emails or messages, aim to trick individuals into revealing sensitive information like login credentials or credit card details. Being aware of the common red flags of phishing emails, such as suspicious senders, misspelled words, and urgent requests for information, can help you avoid falling prey to these insidious scams.

- Social Engineering Awareness: Protecting Ourselves from Manipulation: Social engineering is a technique used by cybercriminals to manipulate individuals into divulging sensitive information or granting access to their systems. This could involve impersonating a trusted source, creating a sense of urgency or fear, or exploiting human curiosity. By being aware of social engineering tactics, we can learn to identify and resist these manipulative attempts.

- Staying Updated: Patching Vulnerabilities and Staying Ahead of the Curve: Software vulnerabilities are constant targets for cybercriminals. Keeping our software up-to-date with the latest security patches can effectively mitigate these risks. Regularly updating our operating systems, applications, and antivirus software ensures that we are protected from known vulnerabilities and can effectively respond to emerging threats. Building a Collaborative Ecosystem: Sharing Knowledge and Fostering Resilience The fight against cyber threats is not a solitary battle; it requires a collaborative approach that brings together governments, industry leaders, and individuals. Information sharing, best practices, and robust cybersecurity infrastructure are essential to building a resilient digital ecosystem that can withstand the relentless onslaught of cyberattacks.

- Government Regulations: Establishing Frameworks for Cybersecurity: Governments play a crucial role in establishing frameworks for cybersecurity, setting standards for data protection, enforcing regulations against cybercrime, and investing in research and development to advance cybersecurity technologies.

- Industry Collaboration: Sharing Intelligence and Best Practices: Collaboration between industry leaders is crucial for sharing threat intelligence, identifying vulnerabilities, and developing best practices to mitigate cyber risks. Sharing information about emerging threats and attack methods allows organizations to better prepare for and counter these attacks.

- Public Awareness and Education: Empowering Individuals to Protect Themselves: Public awareness and education are vital in building a more secure online environment. Individuals need to understand the risks they face, learn to recognize common threats, and adopt best practices for online safety. By fostering a culture of cybersecurity awareness, we can empower individuals to protect themselves and contribute to a safer digital world. The Future of Cybersecurity: Balancing Innovation and Ethical Considerations The digital landscape is constantly evolving, driven by advancements in artificial intelligence, quantum computing, and the Internet of Things. Cybersecurity must adapt to these advancements, incorporating new technologies and approaches to counter the evolving threats.

- AI-Powered Cybersecurity: Leveraging Machine Learning to Detect and Respond to Threats: AI and machine learning are revolutionizing cybersecurity, empowering us to detect threats with greater accuracy and respond to attacks with greater speed and efficiency. AI algorithms can analyze vast amounts of data to identify patterns and anomalies, predict potential attacks, and even automate responses to real-time threats.

- Quantum Computing and Cybersecurity: A Double Edged Sword: Quantum computing, with its unprecedented processing power, holds both promise and peril for cybersecurity. On the one hand, it has the potential to break current encryption methods, rendering our digital assets vulnerable. On the other hand, it also offers the potential to develop new, unbreakable encryption methods, creating a higher level of digital security.

- Ethical Considerations: Striking a Balance between Security and Privacy: As cybersecurity technologies evolve, it's crucial to address ethical considerations and strike a balance between security and privacy. Data privacy is paramount, and cybersecurity measures should not infringe upon individual rights or create undue surveillance. Transparent and accountable practices are essential to build trust in the digital world. The digital frontier is a vast and dynamic landscape, where the relentless pursuit of innovation intersects with the ever present threat of cyberattacks. Cybersecurity is the indispensable shield that protects our digital lives, safeguarding our data, our privacy, and our collective wellbeing. By embracing a multifaceted approach that combines technological safeguards, human vigilance, and collaborative efforts, we can build a more secure digital world, one that thrives on innovation while remaining resilient against the unseen forces that threaten to exploit our vulnerabilities.

Digital Privacy and Data Protection
The digital world has become an inseparable part of our lives, connecting us through a vast network of devices, services, and information. While this interconnectedness offers incredible opportunities for communication, innovation, and access to knowledge, it also raises critical questions about privacy and data protection. In this increasingly digitized landscape, our personal data – from our online activities to our medical records – is constantly being collected, processed, and shared, often without our full knowledge or consent. This chapter explores the complex landscape of digital privacy and data protection, outlining the growing concerns surrounding data collection, usage, and security. It delves into the legal frameworks and technological solutions aimed at safeguarding our digital footprints and empowers readers to understand their digital rights and take proactive steps to protect their privacy. The Rise of Data as a Valuable Commodity The explosion of data has transformed it into a highly valuable commodity, driving the growth of data-driven industries like advertising, e-commerce, and financial services. Companies and governments alike recognize the immense potential of harnessing data to gain insights, predict behaviour, and shape decision-

making. However, this shift towards data-centric practices has also raised concerns about the potential for misuse and abuse. The sheer scale of data collection is staggering. Every interaction we have online – from searching the internet to browsing social media, shopping online, or using mobile apps – generates a vast amount of personal data, capturing our interests, preferences, locations, and even our emotions. This data is then processed and analyzed by sophisticated algorithms to create detailed profiles of individuals, painting a picture of our lives, habits, and even our vulnerabilities. The Perils of Data Breaches and Misuse .The increasing reliance on digital systems has also made our data more vulnerable to cyberattacks and breaches. Data breaches can expose sensitive information like credit card numbers, social security numbers, medical records, and even financial details, leaving individuals and organizations susceptible to identity theft, financial fraud, and other forms of harm. Moreover, the misuse of data can have far-reaching consequences. Data can be used to manipulate individuals through targeted advertising, influence public opinion, or even discriminate against certain groups. The use of data in political campaigns has raised concerns about its potential to influence elections and undermine democratic processes. The Legal Framework of Data Protection: A Patchwork of Regulations. Recognizing the growing concerns about data privacy, governments around the world have enacted laws and regulations aimed at protecting individuals' digital rights. However, the legal landscape of data protection is fragmented and complex, with different regions adopting distinct approaches. The European Union's General Data Protection Regulation (GDPR), which came into effect in 2018, is considered a landmark piece of legislation that has significantly impacted data privacy practices globally. GDPR gives individuals greater control over their personal data, including the right to access, rectify, and delete their information. It also imposes strict requirements on organizations handling personal data, requiring them to obtain explicit consent, demonstrate transparency, and implement strong security measures. In the United States, the patchwork of privacy laws is more fragmented. While there is no single federal law addressing data privacy comprehensively, several states have enacted their own privacy laws, often focusing on specific sectors such as healthcare or financial services. The California Consumer Privacy Act (CCPA), which came into effect in 2020, is one notable example, giving California residents greater control over their personal data and imposing restrictions on the collection, use, and sharing of personal information by businesses. Technological Solutions for Data Protection Beyond legal frameworks, technological solutions are playing a crucial role in enhancing data security and protecting individuals' digital footprints. Encryption, for instance, is a fundamental technology that transforms data into an unreadable format, making it impossible for unauthorized individuals to access or decipher it. Encryption is used to secure sensitive information transmitted over the internet, protect data stored on devices, and secure communications. Privacy-enhancing technologies (PETs), which are designed to enhance data privacy and security, are gaining prominence. These technologies include differential privacy, homomorphic encryption, and federated learning, which enable data to be analyzed without compromising individual privacy. For example, differential privacy adds random noise to data before analysis, making it difficult to identify individuals while still allowing for meaningful insights. Homomorphic encryption allows for computations on encrypted data without decrypting it, ensuring data privacy even during analysis. Federated learning, on the other hand, trains machine learning models on distributed data without sharing the data itself, preserving individual privacy. Empowering Individuals to Take Control of Their Privacy While governments and technology companies are taking steps to enhance data protection, individuals also have a significant role to play in protecting their digital footprints. Here are some proactive measures that individuals can take to safeguard their privacy: Be Aware of Your Digital Footprint: The first step towards protecting your privacy is understanding how much data you are generating and who has access to it. Take the time to review the privacy policies of websites and apps you use, paying attention to what data is collected and how it is used. Control Your Privacy Settings: Most websites and apps offer privacy settings that allow you to control what information is shared and with whom. Take advantage of these settings to customize your privacy preferences. Use Strong Passwords and Two-Factor Authentication: Strong passwords and two-factor authentication are essential for protecting your accounts from unauthorized access. Use unique passwords for different accounts and consider using a password manager to help you create and manage strong passwords securely. Be Mindful of What You Share Online: Think carefully before sharing personal information online. Avoid sharing sensitive details like your address, phone number, or financial information on public platforms. Be wary of phishing scams and avoid clicking on suspicious links. Use Privacy-Focused Browsers and Apps: Explore privacy-focused browsers and apps that are designed to minimize data collection and enhance your privacy. Consider Using a VPN: A virtual private network (VPN) encrypts your internet traffic and routes it through a secure server, making it more difficult for others to track your online activities. VPNs can be particularly helpful when using public Wi-Fi networks. Be Informed About Data Protection Laws: Understanding your legal rights under data protection laws can empower you to demand more transparency and control over your personal data. Support Privacy-Focused Organizations: Support organizations advocating for data privacy and digital rights, such as the Electronic Frontier Foundation (EFF) or the American Civil Liberties Union (ACLU). The Future of Digital Privacy As technology continues to evolve at an unprecedented pace, the challenges of digital privacy and data protection will only become more complex. Artificial intelligence (AI) and the Internet of Things (IoT) are poised to further transform our digital world, generating even greater amounts of personal data and raising new ethical questions. The future of digital privacy will depend on a concerted effort from governments, businesses, and individuals. Governments will need to continue to develop and enforce comprehensive data protection laws, while businesses must prioritize data privacy and security in their operations. Individuals, in turn, must remain vigilant, proactive, and informed about their digital rights and the technologies that can help them protect their privacy. By fostering a culture of data responsibility and promoting awareness of digital rights, we can ensure that the digital world remains a space where individuals can thrive while their privacy is protected. The future of digital privacy is not predetermined; it is shaped by the choices we make today.

Block chain and Decentralized Systems

The concept of decentralization has been gaining momentum in recent years, with block chain technology emerging as a powerful tool for disrupting traditional systems and empowering individuals. Block chain, essentially a distributed ledger, holds the potential to transform various sectors, from finance and healthcare to supply chains and governance. Imagine a world where transactions are transparent, secure, and immutable, free from the control of centralized authorities. This is the promise of block chain. At its core, block chain is a revolutionary technology that enables the creation of decentralized systems. It's a distributed ledger, meaning that a shared and constantly updated record of transactions is maintained across multiple computers in a network, rather than residing in a single, centralized location. This decentralized nature is what makes block chain so robust and secure. Every transaction on a block chain is encrypted and stored in a block, which is then linked to previous blocks, forming a chain. This chain of blocks is immutable, meaning that once a transaction is recorded, it cannot be altered or deleted. This inherent immutability provides a high level of security and trust, making it difficult for malicious actors to tamper with records. The implications of this technology are profound. Let's delve into the key aspects of block chain and how it empowers decentralization:

1. Transparency and Trust:

- Decentralized Nature: The decentralized nature of block chain means that there's no single point of failure, unlike centralized systems that rely on a single authority to maintain records.

- Shared Ledger: All participants in a block chain network have access to the same ledger, ensuring transparency and accountability.

- Auditable Transactions: Every transaction on a block chain is recorded and permanently stored, allowing for easy auditing and verification.

2. Security and Immutability:

- Cryptographic Security: Block chain uses sophisticated cryptography to secure transactions and protect data.

- Immutable Records: Once a transaction is recorded on a block chain, it cannot be altered or deleted, providing a high degree of security and tamper-proof records.

- Consensus Mechanisms: Block chain utilizes consensus mechanisms, such as Proof-of-Work (PoW) or Proof-of Stake (PoS), to ensure that all participants agree on the validity of transactions, preventing fraud and double spending.

3. Reduced Costs and Efficiency:

- Elimination of Intermediaries: Block chain can eliminate the need for intermediaries, such as banks or clearinghouses, in various transactions, reducing costs and processing time.

- Smart Contracts: Block chain supports the creation of smart contracts, self-executing agreements that automate processes and enforce terms, further streamlining operations.

- Automated Transactions: Block chain facilitates automated transactions, reducing human error and improving efficiency.

4. Empowerment and Access:

- Financial Inclusion: Block chain has the potential to provide financial services to underserved populations, enabling them to participate in the global economy.

- Data Ownership: Block chain can help individuals gain more control over their data, promoting digital sovereignty.

- Community Governance: Block chain enables the creation of decentralized autonomous organizations (DAOs), where decisions are made through community consensus, fostering greater transparency and democratic processes.

Applications of Block chain Technology: The applications of block chain technology are vast and continue to expand rapidly across various industries. Here are some of the most prominent examples:

1. Cryptocurrency:

- Bitcoin: The first and most well-known cryptocurrency, Bitcoin utilizes block chain technology to facilitate secure and decentralized transactions.

- Ethereum: Ethereum is a decentralized platform that allows developers to build and deploy decentralized applications (dApps) on its block chain.

2. Finance:

- Cross-Border Payments: Block chain can streamline and expedite cross-border payments, reducing costs and improving efficiency.

- Securities Trading: Block chain can automate and enhance the trading of securities, making it more transparent and efficient.

- Digital Identity: Block chain can create secure and verifiable digital identities, improving identity management and reducing fraud.

3. Supply Chain Management:

- Tracking Goods: Block chain can track the movement of goods throughout the supply chain, ensuring transparency and accountability.

- Provenance Verification: Block chain can verify the origin and authenticity of products, combating counterfeiting and fraud.

- Inventory Management: Block chain can streamline inventory management, improving efficiency and reducing waste.

4. Healthcare:

- Secure Medical Records: Block chain can create secure and tamper-proof medical records, enhancing patient privacy and data security.

- Clinical Trials: Block chain can facilitate the management of clinical trials, streamlining data collection and sharing.

- Drug Traceability: Block chain can track the movement of pharmaceuticals throughout the supply chain, preventing counterfeiting and ensuring patient safety.

5. Voting and Governance:

- Secure Voting Systems: Block chain can create secure and transparent voting systems, reducing the risk of fraud and manipulation.

- Decentralized Governance: Block chain can empower individuals and communities to participate in governance decisions, fostering greater transparency and accountability.

- Land Registry: Block chain can create a secure and immutable land registry, reducing disputes and improving property rights. Challenges and Concerns: While block chain holds immense potential, it's crucial to acknowledge the challenges and concerns surrounding its adoption:

- Scalability: Block chain systems need to be scalable to handle a large volume of transactions without compromising performance.

- Regulation: The regulatory landscape for block chain is still evolving, creating uncertainty and potential obstacles for adoption.
- Privacy Concerns: Block chain's transparency can pose privacy concerns, as transactions are permanently recorded.

- Energy Consumption: Proof-of-Work consensus mechanisms used by some block chains can consume significant energy.

- Cybersecurity Threats: Block chain systems are not immune to cybersecurity threats, and malicious actors may attempt to exploit vulnerabilities.

The Future of Block chain:

Block chain technology is still in its early stages, but its potential is undeniable. It's transforming various sectors, empowering individuals, and creating a more secure and transparent world. As the technology continues to evolve, we can expect even more innovative applications and solutions. The future of block chain is bright, and its impact on society is likely to be profound. It has the potential to revolutionize industries, enhance security, promote transparency, and empower individuals. As we navigate the digital frontier, understanding the power of block chain and decentralized systems is essential for shaping a more equitable and prosperous future.

Chapter Six
Exploring the Final Frontier

Space Exploration and Lunar Bases

The moon, our celestial neighbour, has captivated humanity for millennia. Its silent presence in the night sky has sparked countless myths and legends, and for centuries, we have dreamt of setting foot on its dusty surface. Now, that dream is becoming a reality, as humanity embarks on a new era of lunar exploration with ambitious plans to establish permanent bases on the moon. The allure of the moon is undeniable. It represents a stepping stone to further space exploration, a testing ground for technologies and techniques needed for ventures beyond Earth's orbit. Establishing a lunar base would offer a unique platform for scientific research, resource extraction, and even potential future commercial activities. Recent years have witnessed a surge in lunar exploration efforts. Nations and private companies alike are vying to return to the moon, each with their own goals and objectives. This renewed focus on the moon is driven by a confluence of factors: technological advancements, scientific curiosity, and a growing desire to utilize its resources for the benefit of humanity. The Artemis program, spearheaded by NASA, stands as a prime example of this renewed lunar ambition. This ambitious program aims to establish a sustainable human presence on the moon by the end of the decade, paving the way for future missions to Mars and beyond. Artemis missions will build on the legacy of the Apollo program, utilizing state-of-the-art technologies to explore new regions of the moon, conduct cutting-edge scientific research, and demonstrate the feasibility of lunar living. Beyond the Artemis program, a multitude of other missions are enriching our understanding of the moon. The Lunar Reconnaissance Orbiter (LRO), launched in 2009, continues to map the lunar surface in unprecedented detail, revealing its geology and hidden secrets. The Chandrayaan-2 mission, launched by the Indian Space Research Organisation (ISRO) in 2019, successfully landed a rover on the moon, marking a significant milestone for India's space program. And China, with its ambitious Change's program, has achieved remarkable milestones, including landing the first spacecraft on the far side of the moon. These missions are not merely about planting flags and leaving footprints. They are driven by a scientific curiosity to unravel the moon's mysteries. Scientists are eager to study the moon's composition, its history, and its potential as a source of valuable resources. They are exploring the possibility of utilizing lunar ice for water extraction and rocket fuel production, a key step towards establishing a self-sustaining lunar base. The moon's resources hold immense potential. Its surface is rich in helium-3, an isotope with the potential to fuel fusion reactors, a clean and virtually inexhaustible energy source. Additionally, the moon's regolith, the layer of broken rock and dust covering its surface, contains abundant minerals like iron, titanium, and silicon, which could be utilized for construction and manufacturing purposes. Establishing a permanent lunar base would not be a simple undertaking. It would require overcoming numerous challenges, from developing robust life-support systems to protecting astronauts from the harsh lunar environment. The moon's lack of atmosphere means astronauts would need to contend with extreme temperature swings, harmful radiation, and the constant threat of micrometeoroid impacts. Despite these challenges, the scientific, economic, and geopolitical benefits of a lunar base are undeniable. A lunar base would serve as a scientific outpost, enabling ground breaking research in various fields, including astrophysics, geology, and planetary science. It could also serve as a stepping stone for future missions to Mars and other destinations within the solar system. Beyond scientific research, a lunar base could unlock significant economic opportunities. The moon's resources could be used to manufacture materials, develop new technologies, and even potentially generate energy for use on Earth. Establishing a lunar economy would create new industries, jobs, and technological advancements. The geopolitical implications of a lunar base are also significant. Establishing a permanent human presence on the moon would require international cooperation and collaboration. The Artemis Accords, an international agreement aimed at promoting responsible and peaceful lunar exploration, highlight the importance of shared principles and a commitment to scientific discovery. The dream of lunar bases is rapidly becoming a reality. As technology continues to advance and our understanding of the moon deepens, we are on the cusp of a new era of lunar exploration. The moon, once a distant symbol of human ambition, is now a tangible goal, a stepping stone towards a future of interplanetary exploration and a new chapter in the story of humanity. The moon is not simply a celestial body; it is a symbol of human ingenuity, a testament to our relentless pursuit of knowledge and the boundless potential of our species. As we set our sights on the moon and beyond, we are not only exploring the cosmos but also pushing the boundaries of what we believe is possible. With each new lunar mission, we are writing a new chapter in the story of humanity, a story that continues to unfold amidst the celestial tapestry of our universe.

Mars Colonization and Beyond

Mars, the red planet, has captivated the imaginations of humanity for centuries. It's a world of rusty dust, vast canyons, and towering volcanoes, a stark contrast to the vibrant blue and green of our own Earth. Yet, beneath its seemingly barren surface, Mars holds the potential for life and a new frontier for humanity. The dream of Mars colonization, once confined to science fiction, is rapidly becoming a reality, spurred by technological advancements and a growing sense of urgency to secure a future for humanity beyond Earth. The challenges of establishing a human presence on Mars are formidable. The thin atmosphere offers little protection from the harsh solar radiation and cosmic rays. The frigid temperatures, averaging around -63° Celsius (-81° Fahrenheit), would require advanced thermal insulation and energy-efficient heating systems for survival. And the Martian gravity, only about one-third of Earth's, poses significant challenges to human health and bone density. But the allure of Mars is undeniable. Its potential for scientific discovery, resource extraction, and the opportunity to expand the boundaries of human existence fuels the relentless pursuit of this ambitious goal. The presence of water ice, both in the polar caps and beneath the surface, offers a source of drinking water and potential fuel for rocket propellants. The Martian soil, rich in minerals, could support agriculture and provide materials for construction. The journey to Mars itself is a significant hurdle. The average distance between Earth and Mars is around 225 million kilometres (140 million miles), a journey that could take anywhere from six to nine months, depending on the launch window and trajectory. The spacecraft must be equipped with life support systems to maintain a habitable environment for the crew, shielding them from radiation and providing a constant supply of food, water, and air. The long duration of the journey poses significant challenges to human health, including bone loss, muscle atrophy, and psychological stress. Once on Mars, the first colonists will need to establish a permanent habitat, a self-sufficient ecosystem capable of sustaining life in the harsh Martian environment. This will require a complex system of life support, power generation, and waste management. The construction of such an outpost will rely on advanced technologies, including 3D printing, robotic construction, and innovative materials that can withstand the extreme conditions. A critical aspect of Martian colonization is the development of a sustainable food source. The Martian soil, while rich in some minerals, lacks essential nutrients for conventional agriculture. Scientists are exploring various solutions, including hydroponics, aeroponics, and vertical farming, to grow food in controlled environments using minimal water and resources. Genetic engineering could also play a role in developing crops that can adapt to the Martian environment and thrive in the thin atmosphere. Beyond the immediate challenges of survival, the long-term viability of Mars colonization hinges on creating a self-sustaining society. This involves addressing issues such as social structures, governance, and the psychological effects of living in a confined environment. The challenges of managing a small, isolated community in a hostile environment are unprecedented. The ethical implications of colonizing Mars are also significant. The potential impact on the Martian environment, if any life exists there, must be carefully considered. The long-term consequences of altering a planet's ecosystem, even if it's seemingly barren, are complex and require careful planning and ethical considerations. The pursuit of Mars colonization is not without its critics. Some argue that the resources and effort devoted to this endeavour could be better spent on addressing pressing issues on Earth, such as climate change, poverty, and inequality. Others express concerns about the potential risks to human life and the ethical implications of terraforming another planet. Despite the challenges, the allure of Mars remains strong. It represents a bold step forward for humanity, a testament to our ingenuity and our unyielding curiosity. The successful establishment of a human colony on Mars would be a monumental achievement, a symbol of our resilience and our ability to adapt and thrive in challenging environments. It would not only expand our understanding of the universe but also provide a backup plan for humanity's future, a safeguard against potential threats to life on Earth. Beyond Mars, the future of space exploration holds even greater possibilities. The vastness of the universe beckons with countless opportunities for discovery, scientific advancement, and the pursuit of new frontiers. As we push the boundaries of human exploration, we may discover new worlds, new forms of life, and new resources that could redefine our understanding of the universe and our place within it. The drive to explore is deeply ingrained in human nature. From the early explorers who charted unknown lands to the astronauts who ventured into space, the desire to understand the world around us has been a driving force in our evolution. As we look toward the future, the final frontier of space promises an unparalleled adventure, a journey that will continue to shape our destiny and inspire generations to come.

Technological Innovations in Space Travel

The relentless pursuit of understanding the cosmos has led to remarkable advancements in space travel technology. For centuries, humanity has gazed at the stars, yearning to unravel the mysteries hidden beyond our planet. Now, we stand at the cusp of a new era, where the once-unthinkable prospect of interstellar travel is slowly becoming a tangible reality. This journey has been marked by relentless innovation, pushing the boundaries of human ingenuity. One of the most significant breakthroughs in recent years has been the development of reusable spacecraft. The emergence of companies like SpaceX, with its iconic Falcon 9 and Starship rockets, has ushered in a new era of affordable and accessible space travel. These reusable rockets are designed to return to Earth after launching payloads into orbit, significantly reducing the cost of space exploration. This technological leap has not only opened up opportunities for scientific research and commercial ventures but has also made space tourism a possibility for a growing number of people. Furthermore, the advancements in propulsion systems have propelled us closer to the stars. Traditional chemical rockets, while effective for launching into orbit, are limited by their fuel efficiency. To venture beyond Earth's immediate neighbourhood, alternative propulsion systems are crucial. Ion propulsion systems, for instance, use electric fields to accelerate ions, providing a much more efficient means of traversing vast distances. These systems have been successfully employed on missions like NASA's Dawn spacecraft, which explored the asteroid belt and the dwarf planet Ceres. Another exciting development in propulsion technology is the concept of nuclear fusion propulsion. Nuclear fusion, the process that powers the sun, offers the potential for enormous energy release, far exceeding the capabilities of chemical rockets. If harnessed for propulsion, nuclear fusion could enable us to travel at unprecedented speeds, potentially reaching distant stars within a human lifetime. While still in its early stages of development, nuclear fusion propulsion holds immense promise for future interstellar missions. Beyond propulsion, spacecraft design has also undergone a significant transformation. Modern spacecraft are built with advanced materials and cutting-edge technologies, enabling them to withstand the harsh conditions of space. Innovations in robotics and autonomous systems have allowed us to develop highly sophisticated spacecraft capable of performing complex tasks independently. These robotic explorers have enabled us to gather data from distant planets, moons, and asteroids, revealing hidden secrets of our solar system. The James Webb Space Telescope, the largest and most powerful space telescope ever built, exemplifies the culmination of these technological advancements. Launched in 2021, the James Webb Telescope is equipped with cutting edge infrared imaging capabilities, allowing it to peer through the dust clouds of space and observe the first stars and galaxies formed after the Big Bang. This telescope has already yielded ground breaking discoveries, expanding our understanding of the early universe and the formation of stars and planets. The development of space stations like the International Space Station (ISS) has been another major milestone in human space exploration. The ISS, a collaborative effort by multiple nations, provides a platform for long-duration space missions, scientific research, and technology development. Life aboard the ISS has allowed us to study the effects of prolonged space travel on the human body, paving the way for future missions to Mars and beyond. The innovations in space travel extend beyond our immediate solar system. The quest to find life beyond Earth has fuelled the development of powerful telescopes like the Kepler and TESS missions, which have discovered thousands of exoplanets orbiting distant stars. These discoveries have ignited hope and fuelled speculation about the possibility of finding extra-terrestrial life. As we venture further into space, the need for sustainable space travel becomes paramount. The development of space based solar power systems, for instance, aims to provide a clean and sustainable energy source for spacecraft and potential lunar or Martian settlements. These innovations are crucial for ensuring that future space missions are environmentally responsible and have minimal impact on the celestial bodies we explore. Beyond the practical aspects of space travel, the pursuit of exploring the cosmos has had a profound impact on human ingenuity and scientific discovery. The challenges and opportunities presented by space exploration have led to advancements in various fields, from computer science and materials science to medicine and engineering. Moreover, the sheer grandeur of the universe has inspired generations of scientists, engineers, and artists, driving our collective pursuit of knowledge and understanding. The future of space exploration is filled with promise and uncertainty. The technological advancements we have made in recent years have paved the way for ambitious missions to Mars and beyond, potentially leading to the establishment of human settlements on other planets. The challenges we face, however, are formidable. The vast distances involved, the harsh conditions of space, and the financial resources required for such ambitious endeavours demand significant scientific and technological breakthroughs. As we venture deeper into the cosmos, we must also be mindful of the ethical implications of our actions. The potential for contamination of other celestial bodies, the need for responsible resource utilization, and the implications of extra-terrestrial life discovery all warrant careful consideration. The future of space exploration requires not only technological prowess but also a deep sense of responsibility and a commitment to protecting the environments we explore. In conclusion, the technological innovations in space travel are pushing the boundaries of human ingenuity, enabling us to explore the cosmos in ways previously unimaginable. From reusable rockets to advanced propulsion systems and spacecraft design, each innovation has brought us closer to understanding the universe and our place within it. The challenges we face are immense, but the rewards of unlocking the secrets of the cosmos and pushing the limits of human potential are well worth the endeavour. The final frontier awaits, and we are poised to embark on a journey that will define the course of humanity for centuries to come.

Earth Observation and Satellite Technology

Earth observation satellites, silent sentinels in the vast expanse of space, play a pivotal role in our understanding of our planet's health and the intricate dance of climate change. These sophisticated technological marvels serve as our eyes in the sky, providing invaluable data that helps scientists, policymakers, and the global community monitor and address critical environmental challenges. From tracking the movement of glaciers to mapping deforestation patterns, satellites have become indispensable tools for deciphering the complexities of our changing world. One of the most significant contributions of satellite technology is its ability to provide a comprehensive and long-term perspective on Earth's climate. Climate change, a pressing issue facing humanity, requires a global and holistic approach to understanding its intricate mechanisms. Satellites equip us with the capacity to monitor crucial climate indicators, such as global temperature trends, sea level rise, and the concentration of greenhouse gases in the atmosphere. These data sets, collected over extended periods, provide a historical record of climate patterns and offer insights into the rate and scale of climate change. The role of satellites in monitoring greenhouse gas emissions is particularly crucial. Greenhouse gases, such as carbon dioxide and methane, trap heat in the Earth's atmosphere, contributing to the warming of our planet. By tracking the spatial and temporal distribution of these gases, satellites provide a clear picture of their sources and sinks, helping us identify areas where emission reduction efforts are most urgently needed. These data also enable the verification of international agreements, such as the Paris Agreement, aiming to limit global temperature increases. Beyond the monitoring of atmospheric conditions, satellites play a crucial role in understanding the delicate balance of Earth's oceans. Oceans act as a massive carbon sink, absorbing a significant portion of the greenhouse gases released by human activities. Satellites equipped with advanced sensors can measure ocean temperature, salinity, and currents, revealing the complex interactions between the ocean and the atmosphere. These insights are critical for understanding the role of the oceans in climate change and for predicting its future impacts on marine ecosystems. Furthermore, satellite technology provides invaluable data on the changing state of Earth's ice caps and glaciers. Melting glaciers and ice sheets contribute to rising sea levels, posing a significant threat to coastal communities around the world. Satellites equipped with radar and laser altimeters can measure the elevation and volume of ice, revealing changes in ice mass over time. These measurements offer crucial insights into the dynamics of ice melt and help scientists assess the risks of sea-level rise and its implications for coastal populations. The ability of satellites to capture high-resolution images of Earth's surface provides valuable insights into deforestation patterns and land-use changes. Deforestation, driven by agricultural expansion, logging, and urbanization, is a major contributor to climate change. Satellites equipped with optical and radar sensors can monitor changes in forest cover over vast areas, providing early warning signals of deforestation and identifying areas where conservation efforts are needed. This data is invaluable for policymakers and conservationists working to protect Earth's forests and biodiversity. Satellite technology also plays a crucial role in managing natural disasters and responding to humanitarian crises. Satellites can provide real-time images of disaster zones, enabling rapid assessment of damage and guiding relief efforts. For instance, during floods, earthquakes, or hurricanes, satellites can map affected areas, identify areas of infrastructure damage, and assess the needs of affected populations. This information allows aid organizations to direct resources efficiently and effectively, minimizing the impact of disasters and saving lives. The applications of satellite technology in Earth observation extend far beyond climate change and disaster management. Satellites are also used for a wide range of applications, including:

Agriculture: Satellites help monitor crop health, track irrigation needs, and assess the impact of weather events on agricultural yields.

Water Resources: Satellites provide insights into water quality, identify groundwater reserves, and monitor water usage patterns.

Urban Planning: Satellites are used to monitor urban growth, assess transportation infrastructure, and plan for future development.

Geology and Mining: Satellites provide data on geological formations, identify mineral resources, and monitor mining operations. The growing reliance on satellite data has led to the development of sophisticated data processing and analysis techniques. Artificial intelligence (AI) and machine learning (ML) are playing an increasingly important role in extracting meaningful insights from satellite data. AI algorithms can identify patterns and anomalies in satellite images, facilitating more accurate and timely decision-making. For instance, AI can be used to predict crop yields, detect forest fires, or identify areas at risk of flooding. The future of Earth observation is poised for even greater advancements. Emerging technologies, such as CubeSats (miniature satellites), and advances in sensor technology are opening up new possibilities for monitoring our planet. CubeSats, with their low cost and rapid deployment capabilities, are revolutionizing the field of space observation, enabling a more decentralized and affordable approach to data acquisition. Advancements in sensor technology, such as hyperspectral imaging and LiDAR (light detection and ranging), are providing more detailed and accurate information about Earth's surface. As the volume of satellite data continues to grow exponentially, new challenges arise in data management, analysis, and dissemination. Cloud computing and big data analytics are becoming essential tools for handling the vast amounts of information generated by Earth observation satellites. Efforts are also underway to develop open-source platforms and data sharing initiatives, making satellite data more accessible to researchers, policymakers, and the general public. In conclusion, Earth observation satellites are instrumental in our efforts to understand and address the complex challenges facing our planet. From climate change to disaster management, these technological marvels provide a unique and invaluable perspective on Earth's systems. As technology continues to advance, satellites will play an even more prominent role in shaping our understanding of the world and guiding our efforts to protect and sustain our environment. The future of Earth observation holds immense promise for unlocking new knowledge and driving sustainable development.

The Future of Human Space Exploration

The future of human space exploration is an exciting and ambitious undertaking, filled with potential for both scientific advancement and profound societal change. While current missions focus on lunar exploration and robotic probes venturing to distant planets, the ultimate goal remains to establish a permanent human presence beyond Earth. This aspiration has fuelled a surge in technological innovation, driving progress in areas like spacecraft propulsion, life support systems, and resource utilization in space. Looking ahead, the pursuit of human space exploration will likely be driven by a combination of scientific curiosity, economic incentives, and a desire to secure humanity's future. Establishing lunar bases could serve as a stepping stone for deeper space exploration, providing a testbed for technologies and strategies required for long-duration missions. These bases could also offer valuable resources like helium-3, a potential fuel source for future fusion reactors. Mars, the next logical destination in our cosmic journey, holds immense appeal as a potential second home for humanity. Its geological history, potential for past or present life, and the possibility of terraforming have captivated the imaginations of scientists and enthusiasts alike. Establishing a sustainable human presence on Mars would require overcoming formidable challenges, including radiation exposure, resource scarcity, and the harsh Martian environment. However, the potential rewards are vast: a new frontier for scientific discovery, a backup for humanity in case of global catastrophe, and a unique opportunity to understand our place in the universe. Beyond the allure of Mars, the possibilities for human space exploration extend far beyond our solar system. The discovery of exoplanets, some of which may be habitable, has ignited a new era of exploration. While interstellar travel currently remains in the realm of science fiction, advancements in propulsion technologies like nuclear fusion and antimatter propulsion could one day make these journeys feasible. Such advancements would usher in a new era of cosmic exploration, potentially leading to the discovery of extra-terrestrial life and a profound re-evaluation of our place in the cosmos. The societal implications of human space exploration are as profound as the scientific ones. Establishing a permanent human presence in space could have far-reaching consequences for our understanding of humanity's place in the universe, the nature of consciousness, and the potential for extra-terrestrial life. It could also foster international collaboration and cooperation, as nations come together to address shared goals in space exploration. Furthermore, the development of new technologies and resources in space could lead to advancements in fields like medicine, energy production, and materials science, with benefits spilling over into everyday life on Earth. However, the pursuit of human space exploration also comes with inherent ethical concerns and potential risks. The environmental impact of space exploration, including space debris and the potential contamination of other planets, requires careful consideration. Furthermore, the unequal distribution of resources and the potential for exploitation in space necessitate the development of robust international agreements and ethical guidelines. To navigate these complexities, it's crucial to involve diverse perspectives in the decision-making process, including scientists, engineers, policymakers, and the public at large. Open dialogue and transparency are vital to ensure that the pursuit of human space exploration aligns with our values and priorities as a global community. Looking ahead, the future of human space exploration will be shaped by a confluence of factors, including technological progress, economic realities, and the unwavering human spirit of exploration. The challenges are formidable, but the potential rewards are immense. As we venture beyond Earth, we will not only expand our knowledge of the universe but also gain a deeper understanding of ourselves and our place in the cosmos. The journey is sure to be filled with unexpected discoveries and transformative experiences, shaping the destiny of humanity for generations to come.

Conclusion

As we journey through this era of exponential technological advancement, we find ourselves at a pivotal point in history. Each chapter of this book has explored a different frontier where innovation is reshaping the way we live, communicate, and understand our universe. From artificial intelligence's transformative influence on healthcare and transportation to the potential of quantum computing to revolutionize cryptography and medicine, it is clear that we are only beginning to unlock the vast potential of these technologies.

The rise of sustainable energy, advancements in biotechnology, and the accelerating pace of digital transformation highlight both the power and responsibility that come with these developments. Sustainable energy innovations offer hope for a cleaner, greener future, but they also challenge us to rethink how we use and conserve resources. In biotechnology, the power to edit genes and create synthetic organisms holds immense promise for personalized medicine and disease eradication but also raises profound ethical questions about our role in the natural world.

As we move forward, our understanding and use of these technologies will shape the world in which we live. The digital frontier, with its interconnected systems, augmented realities, and ever-evolving cybersecurity needs, underscores the importance of protecting our privacy and data while embracing the conveniences and efficiencies of a connected world. Space exploration, too, stands as a testament to humanity's innate drive to explore the unknown, reminding us that there is still much to discover beyond our planet.

Ultimately, the future of technology and humanity will be defined not only by innovation but by the choices we make as a society. We must balance our enthusiasm for progress with caution, ensuring that ethical considerations, sustainability, and inclusivity remain central to our path forward. This book aims to provide a foundation for understanding these advancements and provoke thoughtful consideration about how we might harness them to create a better, more equitable world.

As we close this exploration, let us be inspired not only by the possibilities of the future but by the responsibility we hold in shaping it. Each step forward represents a new opportunity for progress and positive impact, as well as a reminder of our shared commitment to leaving a world for future generations that is more just, sustainable, and filled with potential than ever before.

www.ingramcontent.com/pod-product-compliance
Lightning Source LLC
Chambersburg PA
CBHW052330220526
45472CB00001B/354

* 9 7 9 8 3 4 5 3 0 3 5 7 3 *